Super Sewing Series

MARJORIE ARCH BURNS

LINING UNDERLINING INTERFACING

J.B. LIPPINCOTT COMPANY PHILADELPHIA/NEW YORK/SAN JOSE

Printed in the United States of America
ISBN 0-397-40245-7
BICENTENNIAL EDITION

Book design, art, and cover: Ann Atene

This book contains some of the basic principles of the Bishop Method of Clothing Construction from the original texts.

15.7512.1

LINING, UNDERLINING, INTERFACING
by Marjorie Arch Burns
Super Sewing Series

LINING, UNDERLINING, INTERFACING 4

THE UNDERLINED GARMENT 5
what and how much to underline • choosing an underlining preparation/cutting/marking • the underlined dress/blouse underlined skirts/pants • partial underlining • partial underlining for the soft look

INTERFACING TECHNIQUES FOR A COUTURE LOOK 24
interface and underline a neckline • interfacing at front of armhole • the standing collar • rolled collar

THE LINED OR PARTIALLY LINED GARMENT 32
choose a lining • cutting and marking • baste permanent-stitch/press • adjust lining • garment with sleeves/loose lining at hem • loose lining/sleeveless, collarless garment • lined garment with attached hem lined skirt/pants • lined skirt/pants with elastic waistband

IT'S ELEMENTARY 51
preparation/cutting/marking/stitching • stitching guides pressing • pressing guides

LINING
UNDERLINING
INTERFACING

The inner structure is often the factor that gives a garment a particular fashion look. Linings, underlinings, and, sometimes, interfacings may make the difference between a professionally made garment and one that has a "fireside," or homemade, look. Learn the techniques for making these important inner constructions and when and how much to use them to achieve the right fashion look.

Many current fashion looks require a minimum of inner support, but that minimum is important. A deep neckline may need underlining or interfacing; a soft bodice may need support at the shoulders and/or armholes. The skilled sewer needs to know when as well as how much to line or underline. This includes knowing how fabrics and patterns work with the figure, with and without inner support. Jerseys, other soft knits, and Ultrasuede may require little or no underlining or interfacing; but sometimes a tricot lining can be the perfect finish for a soft knit garment.

Use this, the second book of the Super Sewing Series, to learn how—and how much—to line, underline, or interface. There are also ways to make rolled and standing collars, and several couture hem finishes. LINING, UNDERLINING, INTERFACING tells how to make your fashion garment simply and beautifully for a couture look.

THE UNDERLINED GARMENT

Underlining does not show, but it gives a couturiere finish, a look of fine quality, to garments in a variety of styles and fabrics. Underlining controls shape of a garment by supporting structural lines. Because it lies between the body and the outer garment, it absorbs wear and prevents wrinkling. Underlining fabrics are usually soft and smooth in texture. The presence of an underlining adds comfort and pleasure to the wearing of a garment. Underlining also reinforces loosely woven fabric and prevents its stretching. Sometimes interfacings can be eliminated when underlining is used. Couturiere sewing, except for garments and fabrics that require a completely fluid look, is usually done with partial or complete underlining.

Underlining is a second layer of lightweight fabric cut from the same pattern pieces on the same grain as the garment pieces. Underlining and garment pieces are treated as one in garment construction.

Lining is made separately from the garment and attached to it after both have been constructed. Linings and how to make them are discussed beginning on page 32.

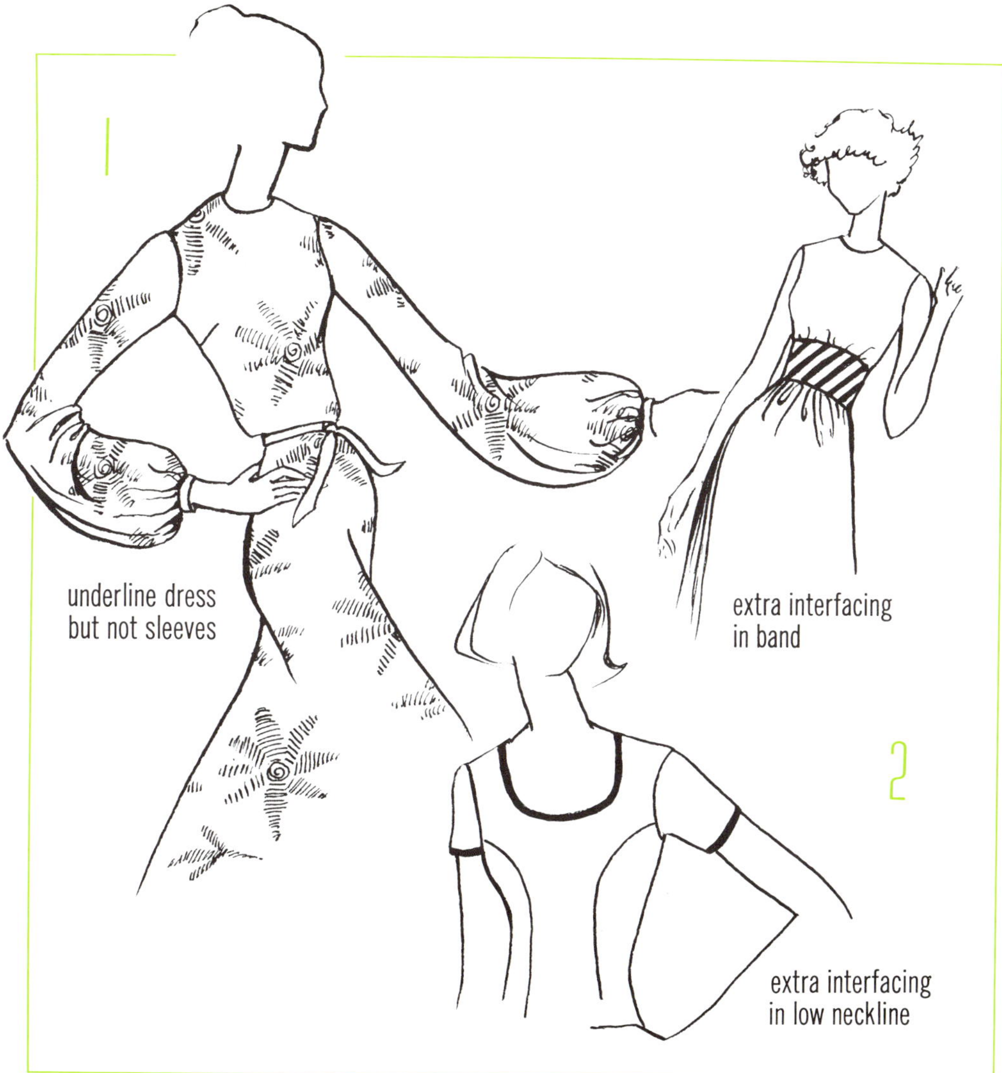

WHAT AND HOW MUCH TO UNDERLINE

Underlining may be complete or partial, depending on the lines of the garment, the look you want, the comfort you require. A dress or blouse usually can be underlined except for the sleeves. If you underline all or part of a garment, you may also wish to line it. (Consider, however, the warmth and additional weight a lining will add.) Sleeves are not usually underlined.

A garment with many pleats, if underlined at all, should not be underlined in the area of the pleats. A garment may require interfacing in addition to underlining in an area requiring added support—waistband or deep neckline, for example. For a very soft look in a hem, bias strips of interfacing may be used at the hemline of a dress or skirt.

CHOOSING AN UNDERLINING

Choose an underlining that complements your garment fabric and will not change its natural qualities. The underlining must have the same care requirements as the garment: It should be drycleanable for use with drycleanable fabric and washable for use with a garment to be laundered. Underlining should be of a weight compatible with the garment fabric. Buy both at the same time, if possible, so you can compare them.

Underlining should not impose itself on garment fabric, except in special cases where the garment fabric requires firm support. For example, if underlining is to be used instead of interfacing to support a midriff section in a dress or to give a crisp line to part of a garment, it should be of a crisp, firm texture that dominates the outer fabric.

You might wish to use different textures of underlining for the same garment. This would depend on the look you wish to achieve. A coat dress front may require an underlining with body and firmness, while the back requires a softer texture of underlining. Study the silhouette carefully, and decide on the look you want. Underlining of contrasting color or with a design is acceptable if the underlining does not show through the outer fabric or affect the outside color. Thread should be chosen for the outer garment, since both fabrics will be sewed in the same seams.

PREPARATION/CUTTING/MARKING

Because of the time and care invested in making your underlined garment you may prefer to dryclean it if the fabric permits. Preshrink wool (page 54) in any case, because steam pressing may shrink it. If you prefer to launder garment, preshrink fabric

and underlining, zipper, and any other notions such as seam binding and trims that will be a part of the garment.

1 It is as essential to keep the underlining as it is outer fabric on true grain. It may be helpful to pin edges of soft or slippery fabric to tissue paper or the cutting board before laying out your pattern.

You may wish to strengthen the pattern tissues for repeated use in
2 cutting both garment and underlining. Lay a plain tissue paper on your pressing board. On it place a thin sheet of plastic (a cleaner's bag that has been cut open, for example). Place pattern tissue on the plastic. Be sure all layers are smooth. Press slowly with a warm iron until the two layers of tissue are bonded to the plastic. Trim off excess paper and plastic but not the pattern margin.

3 If the underlining fabric is slippery you will be able to cut it with a clean edge if you cut it first and with the margin still on the pattern. When cutting add center front and back notches to garment and underlining so they easily can be keyed to perfection when they are stitched.

Transfer all pattern marks only to the underside of the underlining. Place pieces of garment and underlining in units arranged in the order in which you will work on them.

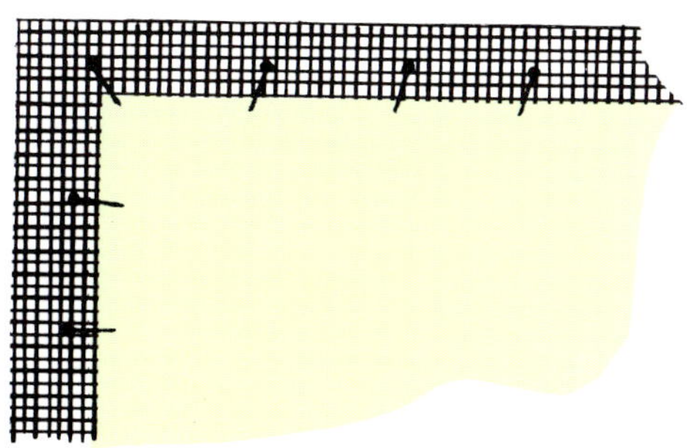

1

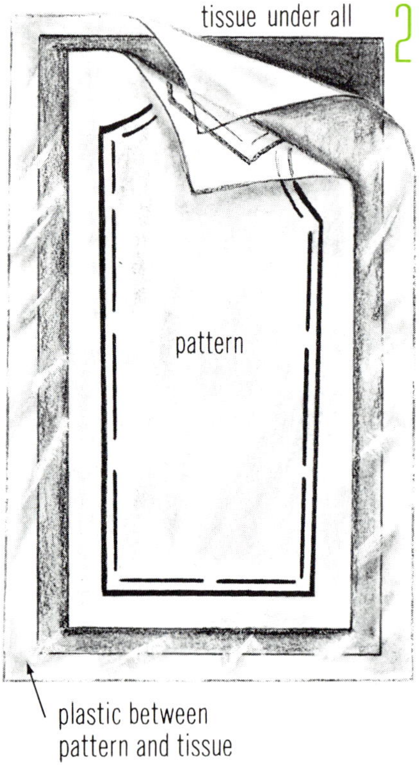

2

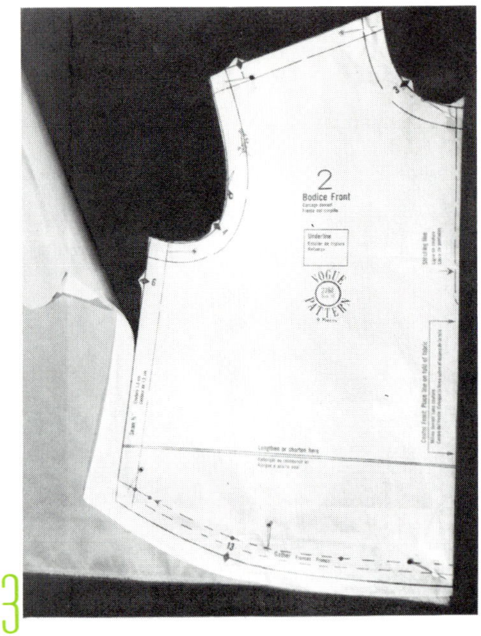

3

THE UNDERLINED DRESS/BLOUSE

PIN UNDERLINING TO GARMENT

As you begin work on a unit, lay the outer fabric on the press board, wrong side up. Press out any creases or wrinkles. Be sure to press with the fabric grain. Place the matching piece of underlining, marked side up, on the garment piece. With the underlining piece on top of outer fabric, press on grain to smooth.

Pin the two fabrics together on center line, lengthwise grain marks parallel to each other.

1 The next step is to key and pin edges at shoulders, neckline, and armholes. Place pins inside seamline at right angles to edge. Below the armhole the layers must be folded together first (with underlining on inside) to allow for turn-of-cloth. (When two layers of fabric are stitched together, the one on the outside must be slightly larger to turn and finish smoothly over the under layer.) Fold or roll the two fabrics on the lengthwise grain along the center front or back line. Carefully smooth any excess underlining

2 toward the side seam allowances. Pin the two layers together. The amount of slippage (excess underlining) will vary, depending upon the two fabrics. There should be the same amount at each seam allowance. On lightweight fabrics there may be none at all. Do not trim off until after staystitching is done.

STAYSTITCH/BASTE UNDERLINING TO GARMENT

If fabric is heavy or bulky, make darts in fabric and underlining separately before stitching the two layers together. In this case you may also wish to insert the zipper in the outer garment fabric alone.

Depending upon the difficulty of handling the two fabrics, you may be able to sew underlining and garment together when you staystitch, or you may find it necessary to hand baste the layers together first in some areas before staystitching.

Staystitch directionally with the grain where you can, but it is more important to maintain control (especially necessary on loose weaves, slippery, thick, or napped fabrics) by staystitching with the firm layer on top, even if you must sew against the grain.

Staystitching is done on all edges that are more than slightly off-grain or require further construction. Place one hand behind the presser foot to help guide the garment sections, and place the other in front of the presser foot to help control the grainline. This will help to keep grainline true when staystitching against grain.

In the photograph the grain threads are pushed out of line. Do not 3
allow this to happen. Control both edges. After staystitching, it
may be necessary to carefully press all edges with the grain to
obtain a smooth seamline. Check the garment pieces to see if the
turn-of-the-cloth allowance has been retained. The two layers 4
should lie smoothly together. Extra underlining at seam edges
can be trimmed away now.

3

4

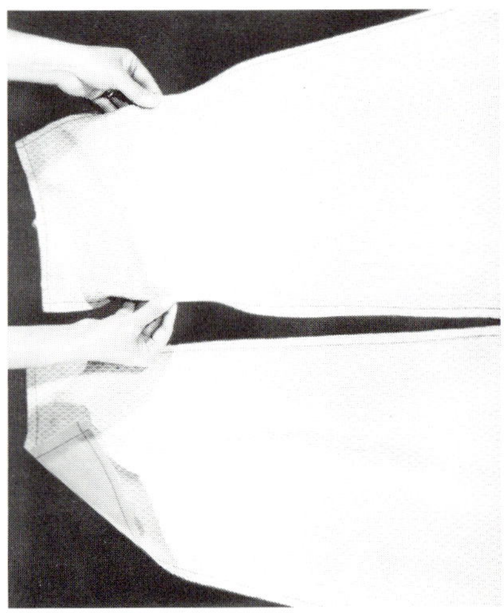

If the fabrics are easily controlled, you can machine baste them together with the longest machine stitch, ⅜ inch (1cm) from the edge. Machine baste only in areas where staystitching is not necessary. Again, stitch in the direction of the grain unless you have more control stitching against the grain. In this case you must stitch with firmest layer on top and control the grain during every inch of stitching as for staystitching against the grain.

DARTS

1 Hand baste the center pickup line of each dart, starting approximately ½ inch (1.3cm) beyond the termination point. Stitch through both layers. This will eliminate bubbles that might otherwise occur. Baste double-pointed (body) darts toward the center from each point. When machine stitching darts through four layers be careful to keep fabric from slipping out of line as you stitch. At this step of construction you may wish to baste the darts for fitting and stitch them permanently after the garment is fitted.

To press darts, place a piece of brown paper between dart and garment. This will prevent press marks on the right side. When darts have been permanent-stitched, slash and press them:

2 ☆ Press shoulder and waistline darts toward center front or center back. Press bustline darts toward the waistline.

☆ Bulky darts (left in photo) may be slashed for 1½ inches (3.8cm) and pressed flat to reduce bulk at seamlines. Wide darts (right in photo) should be slashed open to the point they are ⅜ inch (1cm) wide. At end of slash cut into dart halfway to stitching at an angle.

☆ Trim opened dart seam at an angle for about 1¼ inches
3 (3.2cm) from wide end, ending with ⅛-inch (3-mm) seam allowance at garment edge. This eliminates bulk in seamline.

☆ Clip body (double-pointed) darts diagonally at waistline.

☆ In bulky or spongy fabrics slash darts on underlining to
4 release them if necessary (left photo).

☆ In heavy or bulky fabrics stitch darts separately in garment and underlining before staystitching the two pieces
5 together. On the garment, trim dart away to a ⅜-inch (1-cm) seam as far down as that width on dart. At end of slash cut into dart halfway to stitchline at angle as shown.

Press seam open. Press each dart seam all the way to the point. In point that is not cut open use a metal knitting needle to separate dart when pressing it.

BASTE FOR FITTING

The photo shows a completed underlined dress front unit. Extra interfacing has been staystitched under the underlining. (This technique is given on page 24.) The front is ready to be baste stitched to the back for fitting.

Basting is a temporary stitch; it is done with thread of contrasting color. Use the longest machine stitch. Stitch in the direction of the grain where possible.

The back of an underlined dress may fit better and have a better line if the center back seam is deepened a little, creating a slightly bias seam at the back waistline. See the illustration. Try it with basting first. Later a tiny clip may be necessary at **a** in order for the seam to lie flat.

If the fabric is heavy or bulky you may prefer to insert the zipper in the outer fabric only. If so, you can finish the underlining edge by turning it under and slipstitching it along zipper opening. If you will do this, do not stitch the center back through all four layers for fitting. Baste stitch garment seam and underlining seam separately. Baste in sleeves, and fit garment to your satisfaction.

COMPLETE DRESS UNIT

After fitting dress and making necessary alterations, permanently stitch garment. When stitching use both hands and stitch at an even speed, controlling grain carefully. The underlining on the top layer may have a tendency to push forward, especially on long seams. To prevent this ease the fabric under the presser foot with the fingers of your left hand. It also helps to release the presser foot slightly with your right hand.

In areas where a seam or dart is crossed by another seam, this technique permits the garment to hang gracefully without straining. Sew up to the seam or dart. Stop, lockstitch, and cut the thread. Insert the machine needle as closely as possible to other side of the seam or dart, and lockstitch again. Continue the line of stitching. This keeps the seams and darts that join one another from looking tight and oversewed.

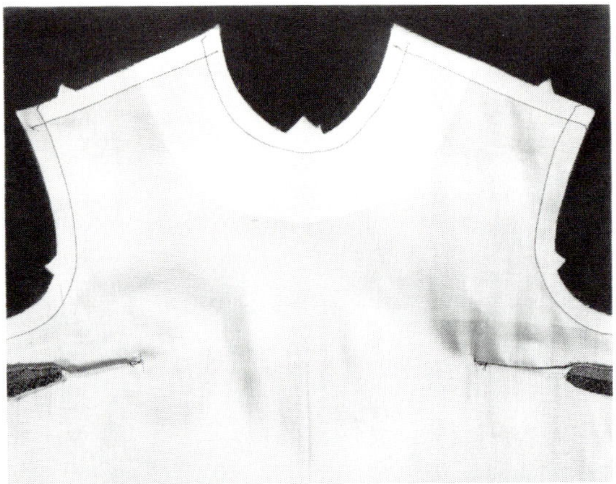

1

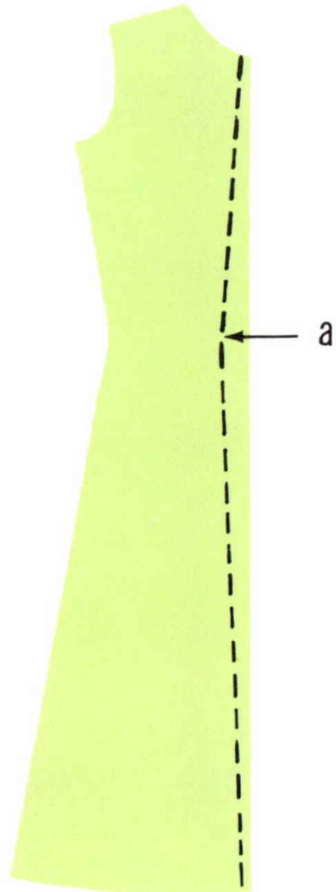

2

If the outer fabric is heavy or bulky, it would be advisable to insert the zipper in the outer fabric only, as indicated on page 14. Apply zipper to one or both layers as required at appropriate time for the style of garment you are making. Apply neck facing or collar. See pages 28 and 30 to apply standing and rolled collars.

Remove baste stitches. Press all seams closed, first, in the direction of the grain. It may be necessary to press some fabrics on both sides of a seam. This helps blend the stitches and smooth all the layers. Then press the seams open. Finish seams in manner you desire or as required by your fabric.

HEM TECHNIQUES FOR UNDERLINED GARMENTS

1 You may prefer to finish your hem before setting in the sleeves. There will be less garment to handle. Before hemming an underlined garment hang it on a padded hanger. Place pins, closely spaced, 1 inch (2.5cm) above the intended foldline, parallel to it. Take garment off hanger, turn hem up, and ease any excess underlining fabric toward raw edge of hem (for turn-of-cloth). Repin

2 and baste the underlining to hem by hand. Trim off excess underlining. Staystitch layers together ¼ inch (6mm) from hem.

Grade vertical seams in hem to reduce bulk. Ease in fullness of lower hem edge by drawing up either long machine stitches or running hand stitches in areas where fullness occurs.

Here are three outstanding ways to hem an underlined garment:

1. Cut strips from underlining fabric on true bias, 1⅛ inches (2.8cm) wide. Stitch to the right side of hem, using short stitches. Stitch ¼ inch (6mm) from edge with hem on top, through staystitching. Fold the end, and lap ¼ inch (6mm).

   3 Trim seam allowance to ⅛ inch (3mm). (The narrower the seam allowance, the more elegant the finish.) Press the bias strip upward. Stitch bias strip in place in well of seam; roll it to the underside as it feeds under the presser foot (see photo). Depending upon the fabric and your skill, you may prefer to do this stitching by hand.

   Hem with a tailor's hem from underside, catching only underlining in stitching. On heavy fabric or with a wide hem, hem halfway up the width of hem, then hem again near top to distribute the weight of hem and avoid pulling on the stitches. This is a double hem (tailor's hem, page 58).

2. For a lace-finished hem prepare the hem edge as already 4 directed to remove the excess underlining and to ease out fullness at hem edge. Select width and texture of lace suitable for your fabric and skirt style. Stitch the lace to the raw edge of the hem, overlapping to cover the staystitching (**a** in illustration) and carefully fitting it. Fold the end under, and lap it ¼ inch (6mm). Stitch lace to underlining only by hand from underside, using tailor's hem stitch (**b** in illustration).

1

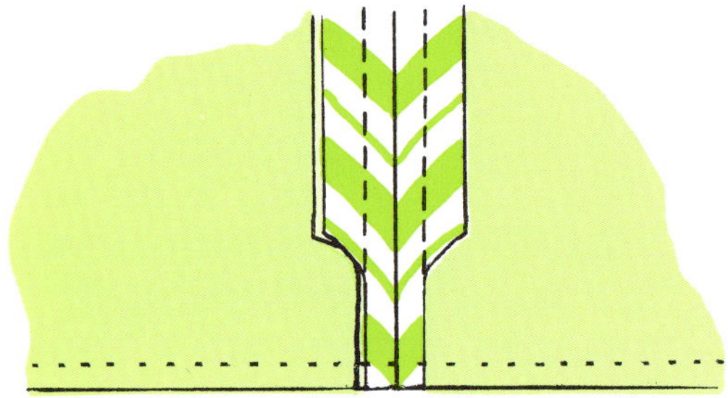

2

3

4

Usually it is preferable not to catch the upper edge of lace as you stitch the hem. Catch it at the lower edge instead. On heavy fabric or with a wide hem, double-hem by hand (see the preceding method).

3. A softly rolled hem is an elegant finish for many garments. Cut a strip of bias 2½ inches (6.5cm) wide. Place it along the hem foldline so that at least ½ inch (1.3cm) extends beyond the foldline into the hem. Loosely catch the bias strip to underlining by hand at **a** and **b** as shown. Use a bias strip or lace to finish hem (1 or 2, preceding). Steam the folded edge in a light final pressing, but do not press it flat.

SLEEVE UNIT

A set-in sleeve should not be underlined. It would be difficult to ease two layers of fabric the amount required for setting in a sleevecap. For raglan sleeves a garment is usually underlined to the shoulders. However, this will depend in part on the cut of the sleeve. See the illustrations. Prepare and apply sleeve to garment as required by sleeve style. Finish it as necessary.

FINAL PRESSING

Touch up only the necessary areas during final pressing. To top press seams and darts, use brown paper or paper towel strips between seams and garment. If the zipper appears overpressed along seamline, turn garment wrong side out, open zipper, and flat press the area under the seamline.

UNDERLINED SKIRTS/PANTS

Skirts and pants may be underlined for several reasons:

- ☆ To give body to a particular line—an A-line skirt, for example.
- ☆ To eliminate the need to wear a slip with the skirt.
- ☆ To make the garment more comfortable, especially if the fabric is rough or scratchy.
- ☆ To help maintain the shape. Underlining gives more support to pants at the knees than does lining.
- ☆ To give more weight and firmness to lightweight, loosely

1

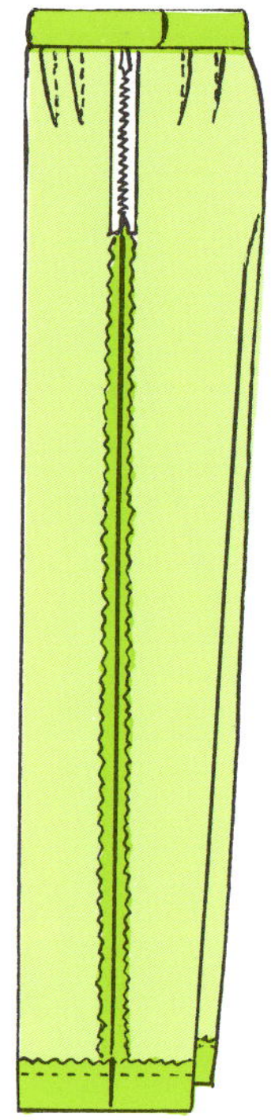
2

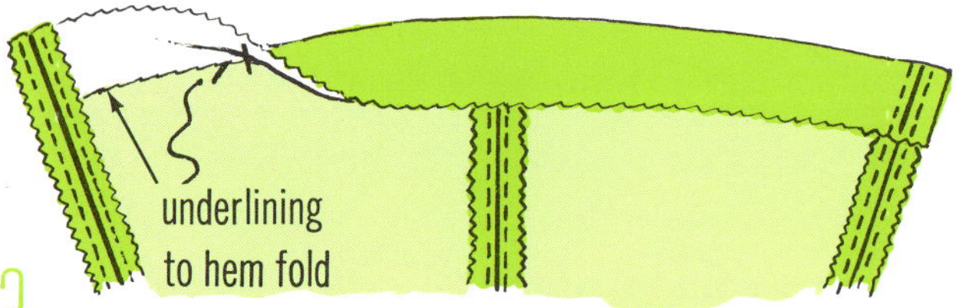

3

woven, or spongy fabrics and to support line of garment.

☆ Underlining is useful if you wish to use topstitching with such a fabric.

Use the methods given for The Underlined Dress/Blouse (pages 9-18) to construct the garment, baste for fitting, and permanently stitch it.

3 You may use any of the methods for hemming an underlined garment given pages 16–18. An additional method that is satisfactory for a skirt or pants is to cut the underlining to the hemfold of the garment. To hem turn the garment fabric to the inside over the underlining and catch edge of hem to underlining with a tailor's hem stitch. Use a double hem for bulky or heavy fabric. Final press as for Underlined Dress/Blouse, page 18.

The color shows how much of these garments to underline. Underline garment or bodice with raglan sleeves to the seams joining sleeves and garment. When a garment has raglan sleeves cut in sections, extend underlining full width of shoulders. Underline only the bodice of garment with square-cut armholes and loose sleeves.

PARTIAL UNDERLINING

With each garment that you make, you will become more skilled in recognizing the extra touches that will make your garment truly outstanding. Study the newest fashions, the latest fabrics, and how the best designers have treated a particular line or detail. Following are suggestions for extra touches that should be helpful.

UNDERLINE ONLY SKIRT OR BODICE

Depending upon the style of your garment, you may underline the bodice and not the skirt, or vice versa. The technique is the same as for underlining separate skirt, preceding.

UNDERLINE ONLY MIDRIFF OR YOKE

1 A dress with a midriff band may require underlining only in the area of the band. This can give greater control to the line of the band, leaving the bodice and skirt soft for a draped look.

2 Underlining can control the crosswise grain of the lower edge of a yoke, back and front, where it is joined to the garment. This may be the only area you need to underline, depending on the garment. This is a useful technique for many yoke shapes.

PARTIAL UNDERLINING FOR THE SOFT LOOK

The fluid look of current fashion requires soft lines for most garments. However, it is still important to hold the line of the bodice firmly at the neckline, shoulders, and armholes. If you do not wish to line the entire bodice or if the garment does not have a waistline seam, use a partial underlining, as follows.

Cut underlinings as shown in illustrations. To maintain the soft, gentle look, do not extend the underlining over the crown of the bust. You can easily trim the lower edge to the correct length for your figure. Staystitch and pink the lower edge. When making your garment use the same construction techniques as for underlined dress or blouse, beginning on page 9.

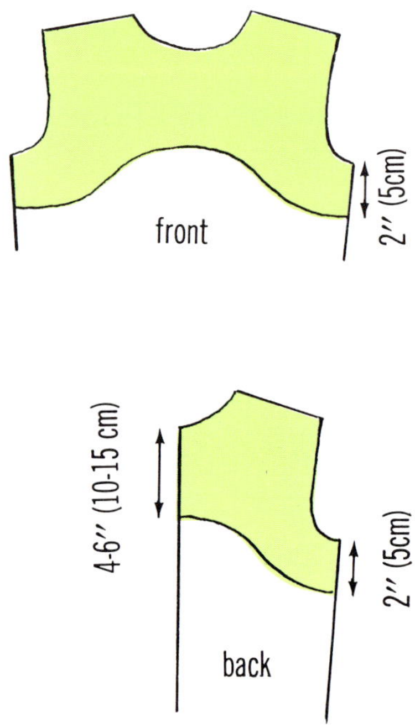

INTERFACING TECHNIQUES FOR A COUTURE LOOK

INTERFACE AND UNDERLINE A NECKLINE

To give added strength and shape for certain styles of neckline and certain fabrics, use both interfacing and underlining. (See photo, page 15. If interfacing is woven it is cut on the same grain as the garment and underlining. Place interfacing between underlining and garment. Staystitch interfacing in place on underside of garment. Staystitch underlining in place. If you are using press-on interfacing, press it to underlining before staystitching underlining to garment.

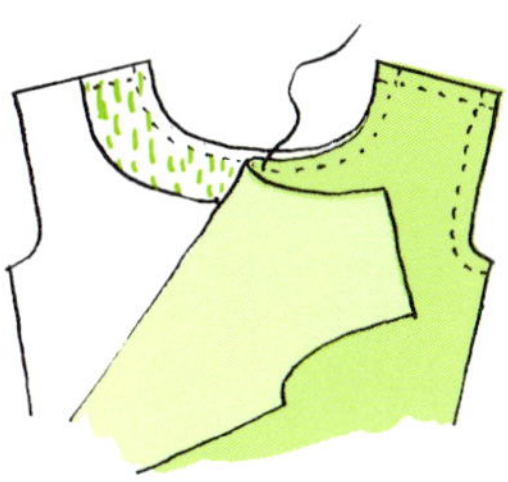

1

2

INTERFACING AT FRONT OF ARMHOLES

Cut a piece of interfacing 1½ inches (3.8cm) wide and long enough to extend halfway up the front armhole. It will give added support to the area, which is useful for certain figures and fabrics. 2
Place the interfacing between the garment fabric and the underlining and staystitch in place. As for the interfacing at neckline, it may need to be held in place by hand basting to staystitch.

3

THE STANDING COLLAR

The standing collar is a fashion look. Two techniques for making such a collar are given here. The first is cut on the bias with a fold at the outer edge. The second is cut on straight of grain with a seam at the outer edge. The effect of a standing collar is determined by the choice of interfacing and handling of collar application as well as by its cut. The depth of the collar should be in 3
proportion to your face, hair style, and neck length. Test your collar by pinning it on the garment and checking it during fitting. Critically examine its depth and fit—how it looks on you.

A BIAS COLLAR

This collar is cut from a double layer of fabric, folded on the bias. The collar is cut on the bias with the fold at the outer edge. Select an interfacing suitable for the desired effect—firm for a crisp, starched-looking collar, less firm for a collar with a soft look. Cut the interfacing, if it is woven, on the bias, too. (Nonwoven interfacings have no grain, so you need not be concerned with grain direction.) Cut interfacing at an angle on outer corners ¼ inch (6mm) inside seamline to reduce bulk. Use one of the following methods to cut the interfacing:

1 ☆ Cut the interfacing the full width of the collar, and staystitch in place along all edges. This gives more body for soft fabrics.

2 ☆ Cut the interfacing along the foldline, and lightly catchstitch it to collar on this edge. Staystitch along other edges.

3 ☆ Cut the interfacing ⅜ inch (1cm) beyond the foldline, and catch it at foldline with invisible stitches that catch only one thread on the right side, and loose large stitches on the underside. This gives the folded edge of the collar a soft look. Staystitch other edges of interfacing to collar.

4 Never press a crease at the folded edge of a bias collar; it will not mold properly at the neckline. With a steam iron shape the other raw edges as much as possible to curve them for the shape of the neckline.

5 Press the ⅝-inch (1.5-cm) seam allowance on under collar to the underside, and trim it to ¼ inch (6mm). This prepares the collar for the hand finishing to be done later. After steam pressing lay collar aside to dry completely. Leave ends of collar open to allow the collar to set properly and for ease in attaching it to garment.

COLLAR ON STRAIGHT OF GRAIN

The collar cut on the straight of grain has a separate under collar. The outer edge is seamed. Use a medium to firm interfacing because this collar stands firmly. Cut the interfacing on same grain as the collar if you use woven interfacing.

adjustment

marking lines

staystitching

hand stitching

permanent stitching

1

2

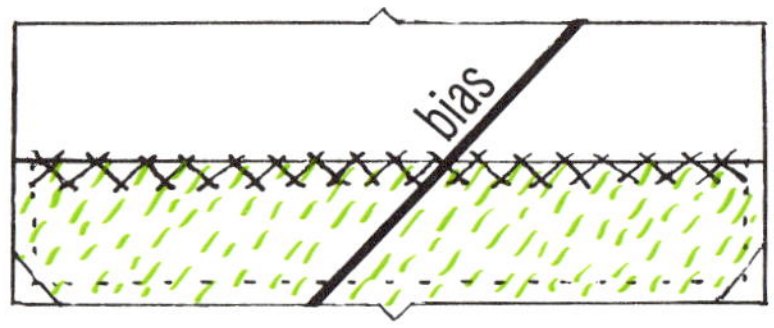

3

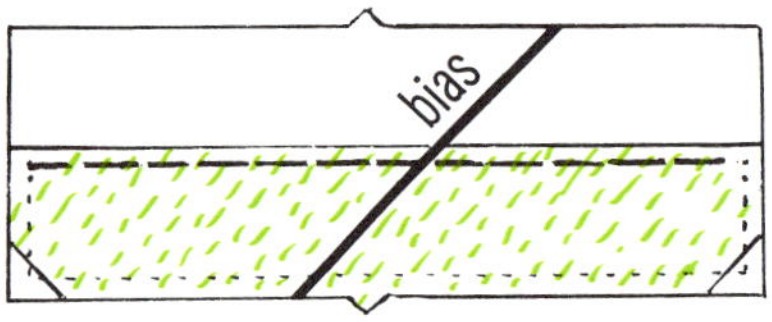

4

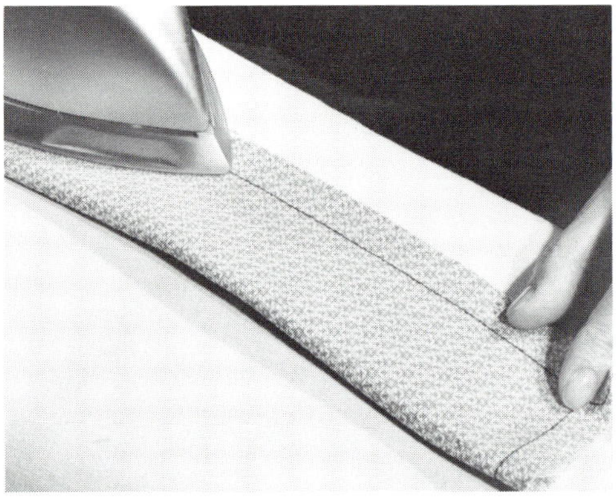

5

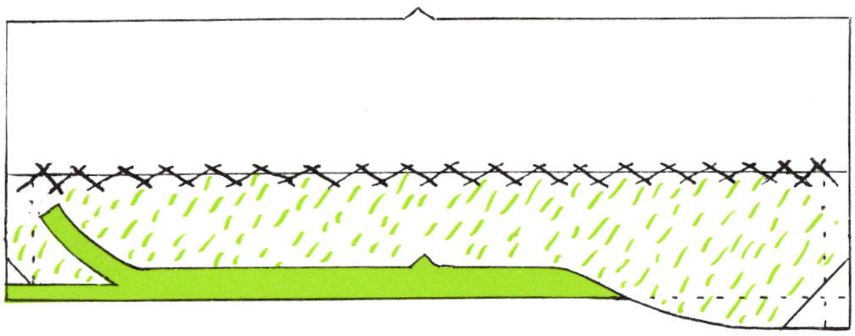

These methods can also be used for collars cut on the straight of grain.

1 Staystitch interfacing to upper collar just outside the seamline in seam allowance. If you use a press-on interfacing, trim away ½ inch (1.3cm) of seam allowance before pressing to upper collar.

2 Trim off ⅛ inch on each outside edge of under collar to allow for turn-of-the-cloth. Stitch top collar to under collar, right sides together, along outside edge. Do not stitch ends. Trim seam to ⅛ inch (3mm) and understitch, beginning and ending 1 inch (2.5cm) from ends. Press, favoring top collar, first from underside, then from top side. Press under ⅝-inch (1.5-cm) seam allowance on neck edge of under collar, and trim to ¼ inch (6mm). This will prepare it for finishing later.

ATTACHING STANDING COLLAR TO GARMENT

With right sides together, key top collar to neckline at center front and back. Pin with the garment on top. This method will make a
3 collar stand properly: Hold the collar firmly for about 3 inches (7.5cm) on either side of center front (**a** to **a** in illustration), stretching the collar slightly in this area. Place this extra ease on either side of the shoulder seam (between **b** and **c**). This gives more fabric at the greatest curve of the neckline, where it is most needed. The notches will not match except between **a** and **a.** The ends are not pinned or stitched until neckline is stitched and pressed.

If the neckline is extremely curved and small, the collar can be attached more easily if the seam allowances on the neck edge of the garment and on the collar are trimmed to ⅜ inch (1cm) before stitching. (A small seam allowance is easier to manage here.

Hand or machine baste collar on garment with the garment side on top. Try on garment and check the stand and curve of the collar. Check set of collar on outer edge. When the collar appears satisfactorily basted, permanent stitch it to garment, again with garment side up. Trim seam allowance to ¼ inch (6mm), and carefully press the seam allowance to inside of collar. Press on a cushion. The seam allowance on the ends may be turned less than ⅝ inch (1.5cm) to make the collar set true.

Pin them, and turn collar to wrong side to machine stitch ends closed. Or if you prefer, use an invisible slipstitch from the right side to stitch the ends closed. Trim seam allowances of machine-

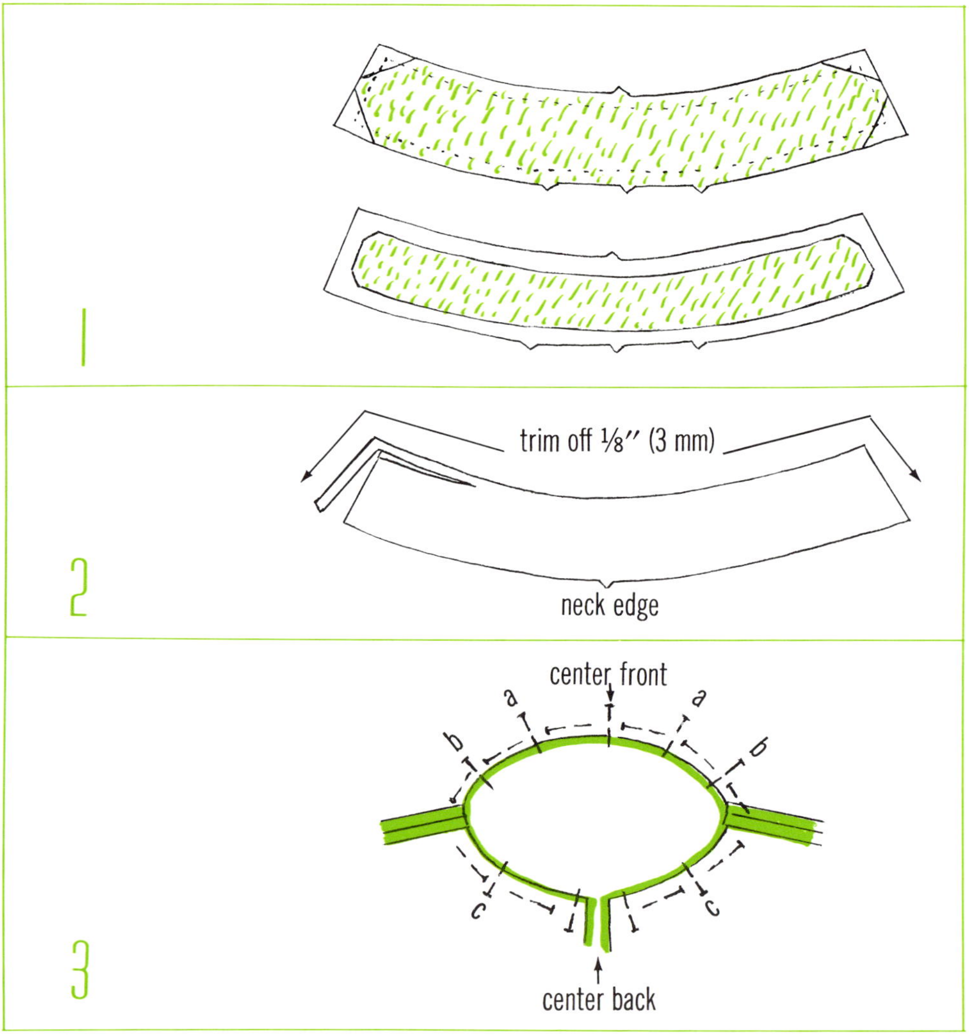

stitched ends to ¼ inch (6mm) for fabrics that ravel easily and are lightweight, ⅛ inch (3mm) for heavy fabrics. Press lightly. Turn and press again.

Turn folded edge of undercollar over neckline and slipstitch to the garment. The stitching must not show on right side. Give collar a final touchup, pressing and molding on cushion if necessary. Two hooks and eyes or two hanging snaps are needed to hold upper and lower edges of collar in place. See page 59.

ROLLED COLLAR

Select interfacing fabric that will complement your outer fabric and give the effect you want. For a soft look choose an interfacing with soft body; for a firm look choose one with a crisp or firm body. Both collar and interfacing (if woven) should be cut on true bias (page 52). Cut interfacing to extend ⅝ inch (1.5cm) beyond foldline. Place interfacing on wrong side of under collar with ⅝ inch (1.5cm) overlapping the foldline, as shown. Trim lower corners ¼ inch (6mm) beyond seamline, at an angle.

Hand stitch interfacing to collar ½ inch (1.3cm) from edges. At foldline take invisible hand stitches from right side and long, loose stitches on underside. (Because collar is cut on bias, machine staystitching might distort the grain.) Do not press the bias fold of the collar. Let it fall into place.

The secret of a couturiere look in a rolled collar is to use the correct amount of ease in the proper area. With bulky or stiff fabrics and on deep curves trim seam allowance on neck edges of garment and collar to ⅜ inch (1cm) for ease in applying collar. It is always easier to work with and stitch a seam with a narrow seam allowance when stitching on a deep curve.

With right side of garment and collar together, match the collar and neckline center fronts and center backs; pin. To make this collar roll properly, stretch collar, without really pulling it, toward front at both shoulder seams. Place the greatest amount of ease 1½ inches (3.8cm) on each side of neck edge, at center front. See illustration. This application permits the collar to roll down and conceal the neckline seam. Stitch collar to neck edge, garment side up. Trim seam allowance to ¼ inch (6mm), and press up.

Roll the collar ends over your fingers, permitting the top collar to shape and set. Shape the turn of the collar at both ends as well. Stretch the foldline slightly if necessary, so collar rolls down over the neckline seam. Always favor the side of collar that will show.

Pin to hold roll line. Pin each end of collar in two places—the two upper layers, at **b,** and the two under layers, at **c,** together on each side. Close ends with fine hand stitches. This method will prevent the ends from turning up because you can favor the collar as needed to set properly. Trim remaining seam allowance to ¼ inch (6mm), turn under, and pin in position so it is not twisted or pulled off grain. Slipstitch (page 59) to inside of garment neckline. To reduce the bulk in the seamline this edge may be staystitched and overcast before stitching in place if fabric is heavy, stiff, or if it is a double knit. 3

Hang garment on hanger or place on dress form. Steam collar, and shape the roll line with your hands. Use two hooks and eyes or two hanging snaps (page 59) to hold collar in place. 4

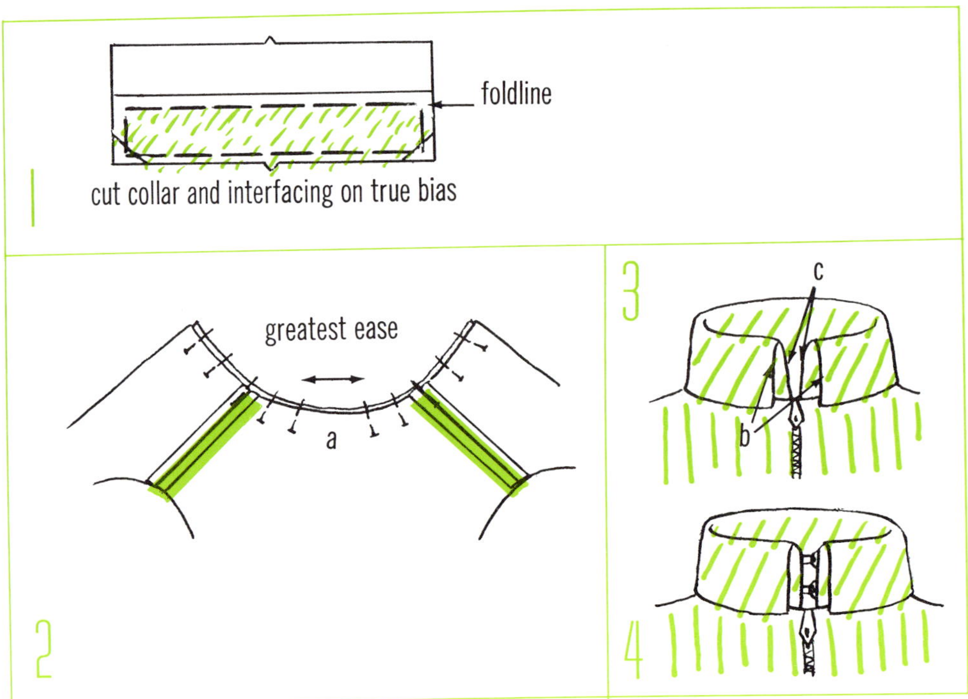

THE LINED OR PARTIALLY LINED GARMENT

Linings add elegance to garments, make garments more comfortable to wear, and eliminate the necessity for seam finishes inside garments; they protect the skin from rough outer fabrics. There are other advantages. A lined garment wrinkles less during wear. A lined knit garment clings less. Lining a garment is easier and less time-consuming than underlining one.

For example, sewing the seams in both garment and lining would not be as time-consuming as finishing seams, hems, and facings in an underlined garment. Lining is also much easier for the average sewer to handle than underlining.

Depending on their construction, garments may be partially lined. In the illustrations the bodice but not the skirt of the full-skirted jumper would be lined. In the dress with peplum, the bodice but not the peplum would be lined. Line the jacket of the pants suit, but not the pants. This makes the jacket easier to take off and to put on. The lining is particularly desirable in a jacket of this open style. The sleeves need not be lined. The bodice of the low-cut, empire-style dress would be much more attractive lined than if facings were used in the small areas of neckline and armholes.

CHOOSE A LINING

Lining fabric should be smooth, lightweight, and have the same care requirements—laundry or drycleaning—as the garment fabric. The lining fabric should not cling or create bulk. Contrasting color or print can be attractive and adds a special touch, so long as it does not show through the outer garment fabric. Lightweight dress fabrics can be used as linings. Tricot or knit linings are often used in knit dresses or pants tops. They prevent outer knit fabric from clinging, help conceal figure faults, and they move and give with the outer fabric.

You may wish to underline your garment and line it, too. Consider the weight and warmth that will be added to the garment in this way, however. This might be done for a dress or a skirt.

CUTTING AND MARKING

Consider additional uses for your lining. In a sleeveless garment without a collar, lining can replace neckline and/or armhole facings, becoming an all-in-one finish. Cut the lining the same as the garment except for length. In a garment with sleeves but no collar the lining can serve as the neckline finish and replace the facing.

However, in both cases, if a facing is needed to give more body to neckline and/or armholes or if it is needed to conceal a lining of a different color, use one. It is applied over the lining. In this instance the lining acts as a kind of interfacing at the neckline and/or armholes; or it can be trimmed and stitched to the edge of the facing if it creates too much bulk. 3

Lining may be staystitched into the armholes, or it may be finished separately. This will depend on the fabric, the desired firmness at the armholes, and your figure. For a garment with a collar the lining may be treated in any of the preceding ways most suitable for the fabric and style. Lining can be finished two ways at the hemline. First, the hems can be left loose and finished separately. The second technique eliminates a hem finish for garment and lining, but it is not so easy for the novice: The hems can be attached at the hemline (pages 44–46). Select the method best suited for your fabric and garment. Prepare your fabric to maintain grain perfection, and preshrink if necessary (pages 53–54). 4

If either fabric is slippery, do not trim the margin from the pattern, and cut the slippery fabric first. If the margin has already been trimmed and the slippery fabric is difficult to handle, place a sheet of tissue paper above or below the fabric before pinning the pattern. The tissue will keep the fabric from slipping as you cut.

All of the lining pieces should be cut and marked the same way as the garment pieces, with the following exceptions:

1 ☆ For a loose lining at the hem the lining is cut 1 inch (2.5cm) shorter than the garment. Both will have hems the same width, so the lining will finish 1 inch (2.5cm) shorter than the garment. If the dress has a hem of 1½ inches (3.8cm) or less, cut lining to the finish length plus 1 inch (2.5cm). (The narrow garment hem does not give the depth for a take-up tuck, and the lining could pull on the bottom of the dress otherwise.)

2 ☆ If the lining will be attached at the hem, cut it to the hem foldline (the length the garment will be finished). One-eighth inch (3mm) must be cut from lining armholes and neckline for turn-of-cloth if lining is used as facing.

3 ☆ If lining will be attached to edges of facings (as in jacket or coat style dress), cut it this way: Place facing pattern on garment pattern, and mark edge **a** of facing pattern. Remove facing pattern, and mark ⅝ inch (1.5cm) toward neckline from mark at facing edge, **b.** This will be the cutting line for the lining. A ¼-inch (6-mm) seam allowance for attaching the lining to the facing is now included. Use the same technique anywhere there is a facing on a garment and you want to attach lining to facing. Lining can be stitched to facing by Method One or Method Two, pages 44–46.

☆ Sleeves in dresses and tops are not usually lined, so you will not need to cut these.

Mark all garment and lining pieces, and place in units of work.

BASTE FOR FITTING

Staystitch, directionally, garment pieces where they require it (pages 56, 57). Stitch darts unless they need to be fitted; if so, baste them. Baste seams directionally for fitting. Prepare and baste in the sleeves. The lining should not be stitched or put in garment

1

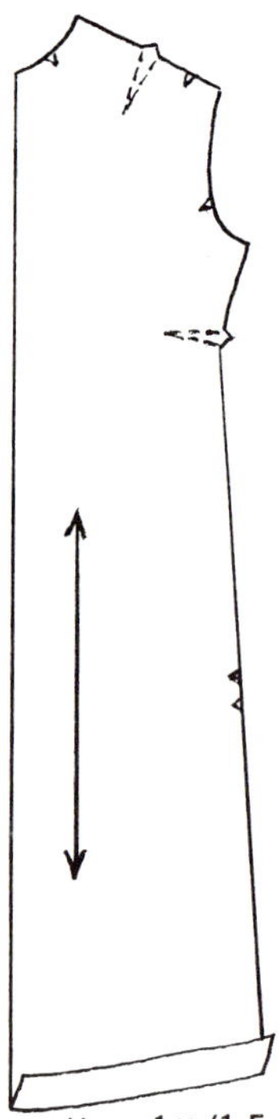

turn up pattern 1″ (1.5 cm)
to cut lining

2

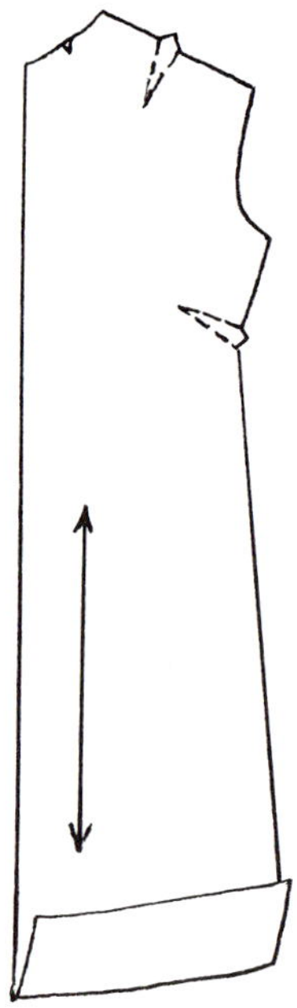

turn up pattern
on hem foldline
to cut lining

trim ⅛″ (3 mm)
from lining
neckline and
armholes

3

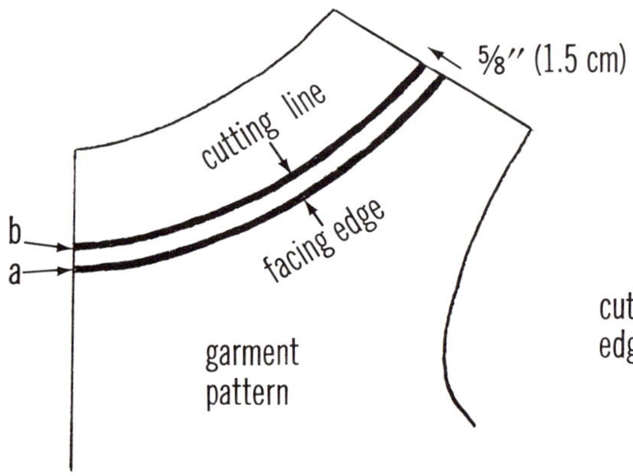

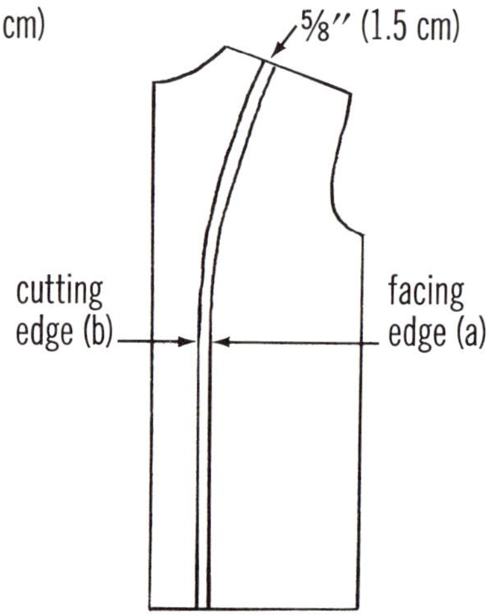

until the fitting has been completed to your satisfaction. Fit garment. Make notes of all corrections because the same adjustments will be necessary for the lining.

PERMANENT-STITCH/PRESS

Remove basted sleeves from garment. Permanent-stitch all seams and darts, and remove basting threads. Press darts and seams as you go. Insert zipper in desired manner. (The sleeveless dress on pages 42–44 is an exception.) It is important to take special care with pressing while lining and garment are separate. After lining has been inserted it is difficult to press garment well.

ADJUST LINING

Remember that the lining will be inserted with its wrong side to the wrong side of the garment. For this reason adjustments made on the garment will need to be made on the opposite side of the lining. For example, if the right seam was adjusted on the garment, the same adjustment must be made on the left seam of the lining. Press darts in lining in the opposite direction you pressed them in garment. This distributes the bulk. Turn under and press the center back or front seam allowances at the garment opening.

GARMENT WITH SLEEVES/LOOSE LINING AT HEM

HEMS

Finish hems on garment and lining in desired manner. Make both the same width. The lining will finish 1 inch (2.5cm) shorter than the garment because it was cut 1 inch (2.5cm) shorter. This keeps the lining from showing when you wear the garment. Place lining in garment with the wrong sides together. Key garment and lining at center fronts and backs, and pin. (See photos, 1, page 45.)

ARMHOLES

If lining is needed at armholes to give body, staystitch lining and garment together here. Sew in sleeves. If lining is to be kept free at

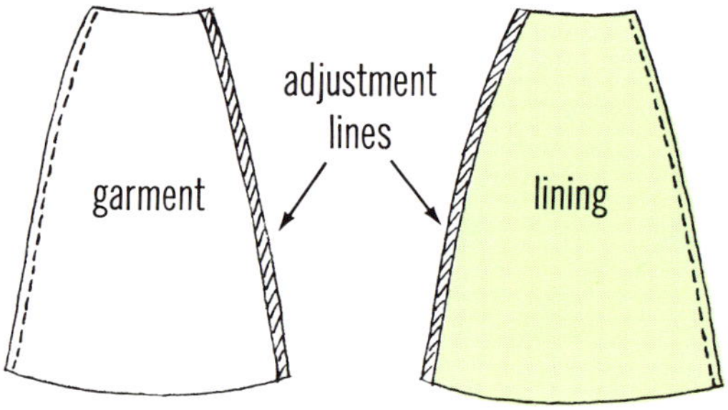

1

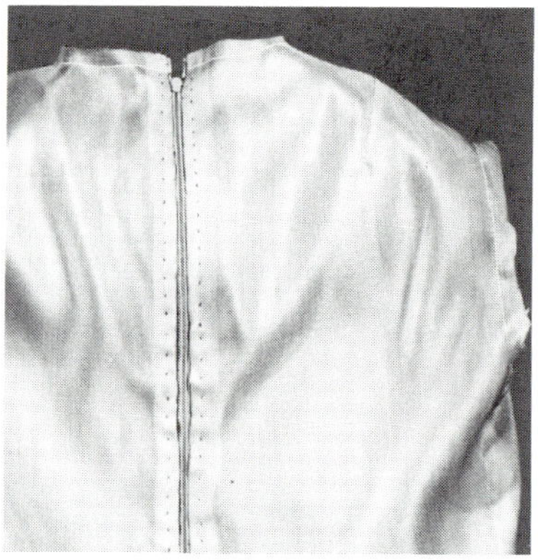

2

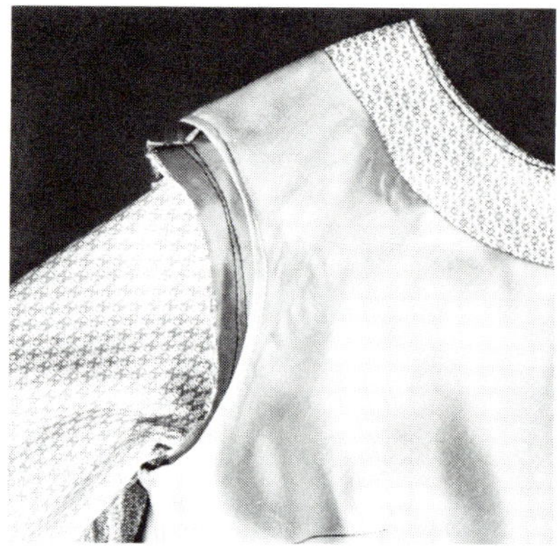

3

armholes, sleeves can be stitched in before inserting lining. Trim ¾ inch (2cm) from lining armholes. Finish armholes of lining with seam binding (Hong Kong finish), or use a narrow rolled hem if the fabric is not bulky and rolls easily. 3

NECKLINE

If the garment has a collar and/or if a facing will be used over the lining, staystitch the lining and garment together at neckline. If a facing is used over the lining, the lining acts as an interfacing in this area. If the lining will be attached to the edge of facing, follow instructions on page 44 or page 46.

LINING AT ZIPPER

The lining seam allowances have been pressed under ⅝ inch (1.5cm) at the garment opening. Whipstitch this folded edge to zipper tape, keeping the lining ⅛ inch (3mm) from zipper teeth. A second row of stitching may be used ¼ inch (6mm) away from the first to prevent the lining from catching in zipper (photo 2, page 39).

LOOSE LINING/SLEEVELESS, COLLARLESS GARMENT

METHOD ONE

This method can be used on any collarless, sleeveless garment 1
that has two side seams and a center front or back seam. The shoulders should be at least 1½ inches (3.8cm) wide because the lining will be turned through the shoulders. The lining also will serve as a one-piece armhole and neckline facing.

After the garment has been fitted, sew all darts and seams per- 2
manently. Press, but do not sew the side seams or insert the zipper. Prepare lining in same steps as dress. Sew and press all but the center back and side seams. Trim ⅛ inch (3mm) from neckline and armholes to allow for turn-of-cloth. Neither lining nor garment has been hemmed.

With right sides together, pin lining to garment, carefully matching notches, center front or back seams, shoulder seams, neckline corners and armholes. With garment side up machine stitch neckline and armholes, using small stitches. Lockstitch, and cut threads. Keep checking as you sew to be sure lining and garment fabrics are moving under presser foot at the same rate. Press seams flat. Trim allowances to ⅛ inch (3mm) and understitch.

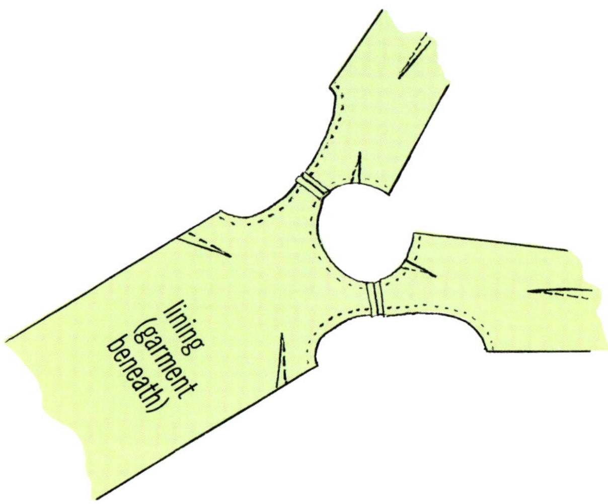

2

Turn garment right side out through shoulders: Working through each shoulder seam, carefully pull the corresponding part of lining and garment through to right side. Carefully press edges, favoring garment side. Insert zipper in garment in standard way.

To join side seams of garment and lining, work on one side of garment at a time. Pin garment front and garment back, right sides together, at side seams, matching notches. Be careful to keep the armholes matched at underarm. Pin lining front and back together in same way. Starting at the hem edge, stitch side seams of garment to 1 inch (2.5cm) beyond underarm seam at armhole. Lockstitch and cut threads. Starting from hem edge of lining, join side seam up to the first stitching line on garment. Repeat procedure on other side seams of garment and lining. Fasten lining with hand or machine stitches to one side of seam allowance. Sew center back seam of lining to zipper opening. Fasten lining to zipper tape as shown on page 43. Complete hems separately on garment and lining.

METHOD TWO

This method is used on a garment without a center front or back seam or on a garment in which the zipper has been inserted—a garment that cannot be turned through the shoulders. It can also be used if the lining is attached at lower edge. (See next section.) All seams are stitched and pressed.

2 Stitch necklines of garment and lining, right sides together, after
keying them at shoulder seams, center fronts and backs. Under-
stitch, turn, and press. Turn under and key shoulder seam allow-
3 ances of garment and lining at armholes as shown. Pin to hold
keyed position. From the inside pull front armhole seam of gar-
ment and lining to the inside. Reposition key pin to inside at
4 shoulder seam. Key edges, and stitch front armhole of garment to

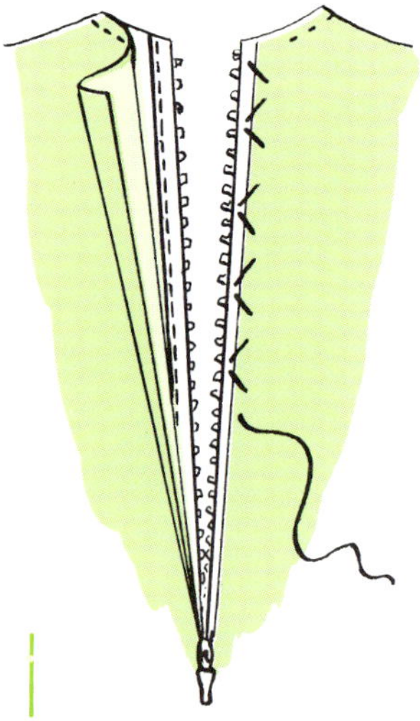

1

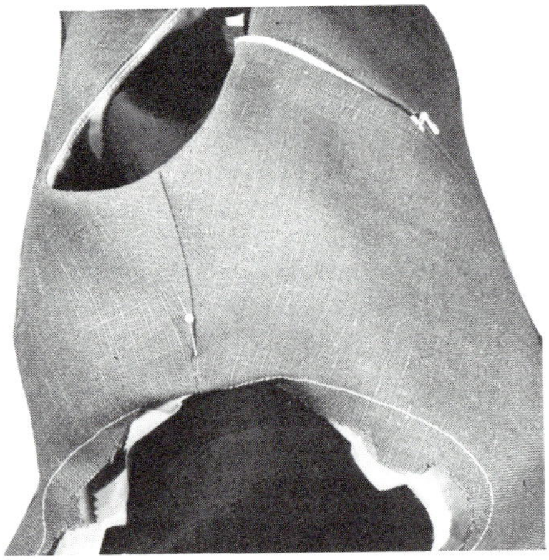

3

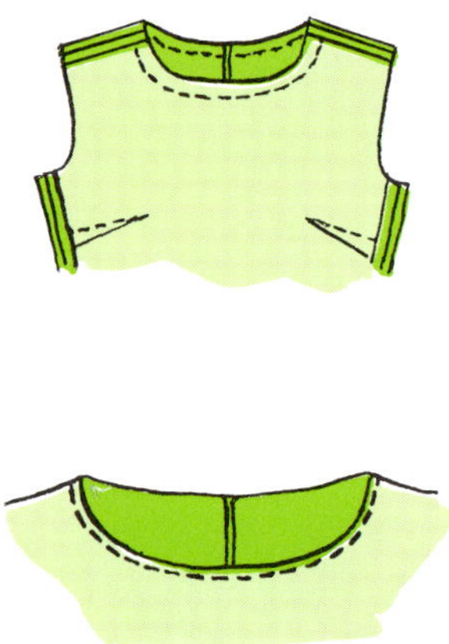

neckline trimmed,
turned, and
understitched

2

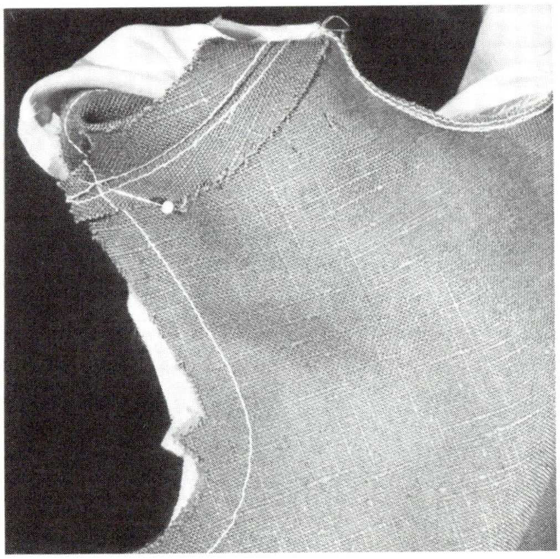

4

front armhole of lining. (You will be able to sew only one-half the armhole at a time.) After stitching front armhole, repeat procedure for back. Trim seams to scant ¼ inch (6mm). Understitch armhole in two steps, by hand or by machine. Repeat entire procedure for second armhole.

1 Finish hems of garment and lining separately. The photos show two completed garments with loose linings and a variety of hem finishes.

LINED GARMENT WITH ATTACHED HEM

Insert zipper. If lining is to be free at armholes, complete neckline
2 facing, and sew in sleeves. Turn up and press hem in garment. Prepare hem edge by staystitch plus or ease stitching, but do not stitch it in place.

The lining is inserted in garment starting at hem and working upward. Key and pin all seams at hem matching raw edges of lin-
3 ing to dress, right sides together. Use a fine, running hand stitch or a long machine stitch to join lining to garment around entire hem. Next, handstitch hem in place with tailor's hem. The excess lining is lightly pressed, usually without steam, into a takeup tuck.

Pull lining over garment, wrong sides together. Finish armholes of garment in the same way as for garment with loose lining, page 38. (In that case the neckline was stitched closed, and the hemline was open. Here the positions are reversed, but the same principle can be used.) The two following methods can be used to attach the lining to neckline facing.

METHOD ONE

4 The neckline facing should be completed, but not finished at outer edges. Staystitch edge of facing and edge of lining at ¼ inch (6mm).

Key raw edge of lining to facing edge, right sides together, and
5 stitch them ¼ inch (6mm) from edges. (Turn to wrong side through front or back opening.) Clip to staystitching on lining if necessary to key it to the curve of facing. The stitching may be done by hand or by machine. Turn garment, and press lining in place.

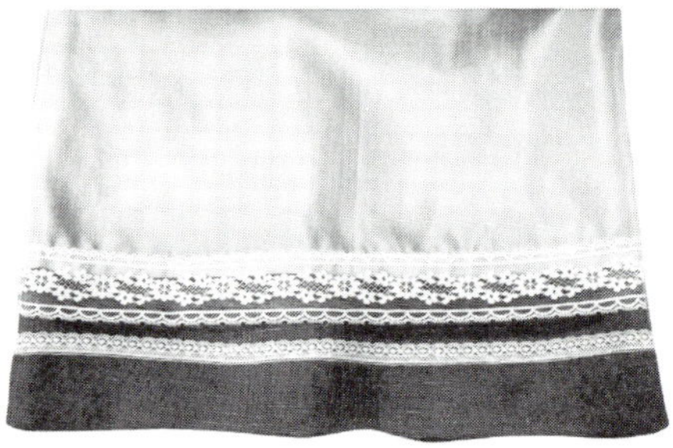

1

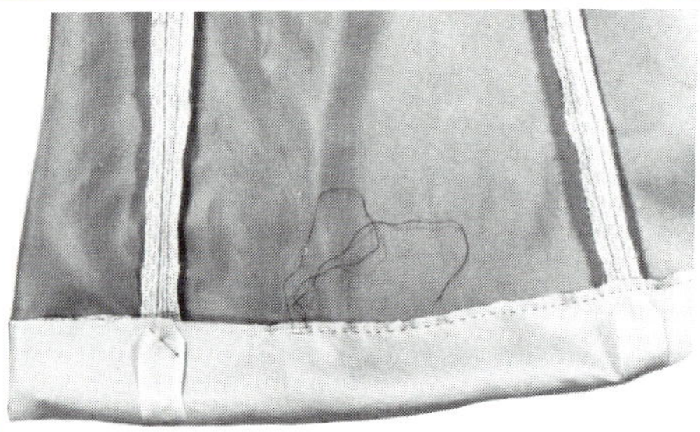

2

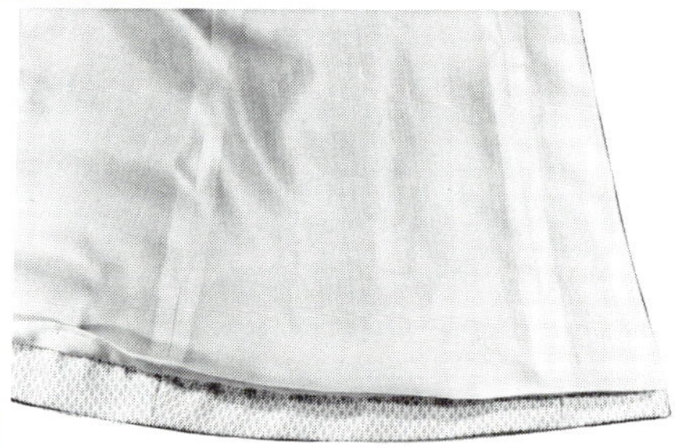

3

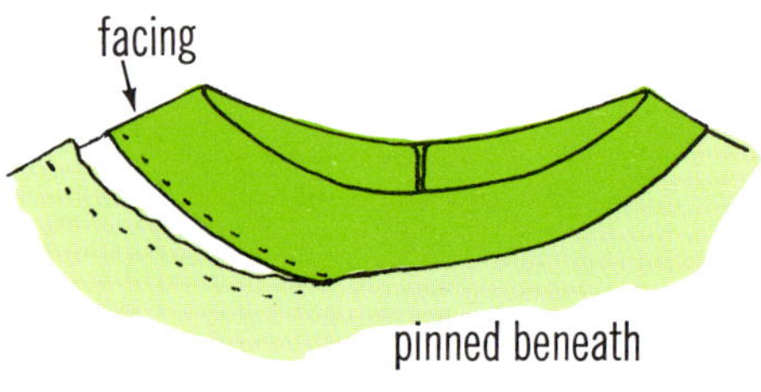
facing
pinned beneath

4

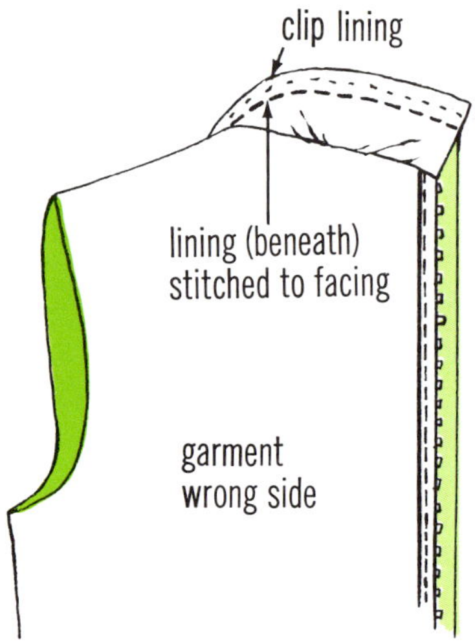
clip lining
lining (beneath)
stitched to facing
garment
wrong side

5

METHOD TWO

Instead of turning garment and lining to stitch from the inside you
1 may prefer to whipstitch lining to facing by hand. To do so, stay-
stitch facing and lining ¼ inch (6mm) from edges. Clip to stay-
stitching where necessary to turn lining under on staystitching line
¼ inch (6mm). Pin to staystitching on facing, and whipstitch in
place by hand. Lightly press facing and lining, usually without
steam.

LINED SKIRT/PANTS

Lining a skirt or pants is basically the same as lining any other garment. Note the following points, however:

☆ When the zipper is in a side seam, be sure the leave the lining zipper opening in the opposite side from the garment. (This is because the wrong sides of garment and lining will be stitched together.)

☆ It is usually better to hem the zipper area of the lining
2 separately. Staystitch the opening on the seamline. Stay-
stitch a second row in the seam allowance, ¼ inch (6mm)
from the first. Press seam allowance to wrong side, and turn
raw edge under on second line of staystitching. Topstitch
opening along folded edge. Stitch back and forth across
lower edge of opening to reinforce it.

☆ Press darts in lining the opposite direction from those in the garment.

3 ☆ For a full skirt it may be more satisfactory to make a rolled
hem. Machine stitch it, and finish the outside or both sides
with lace. To do this, cut the lining ½ inch (1.3cm) shorter
than the length the garment is to be finished.

staystitching -

hand stitching — — — — — — — — — — — — — — — —

permanent stitching ------------------------------

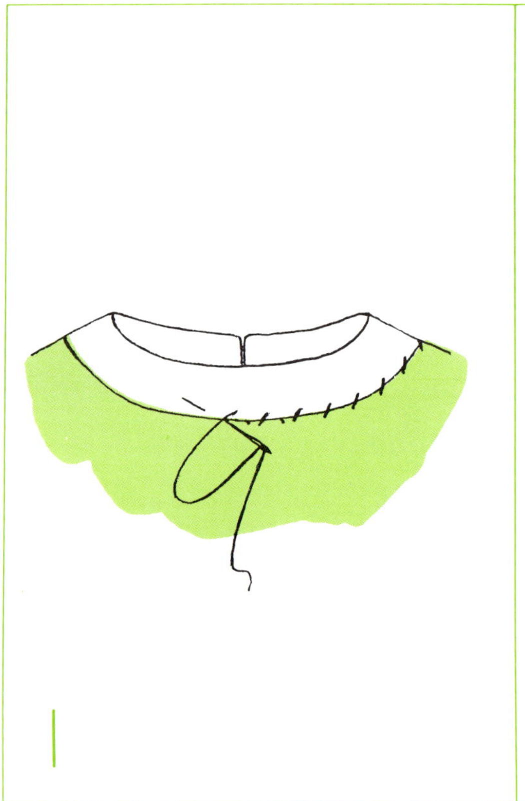

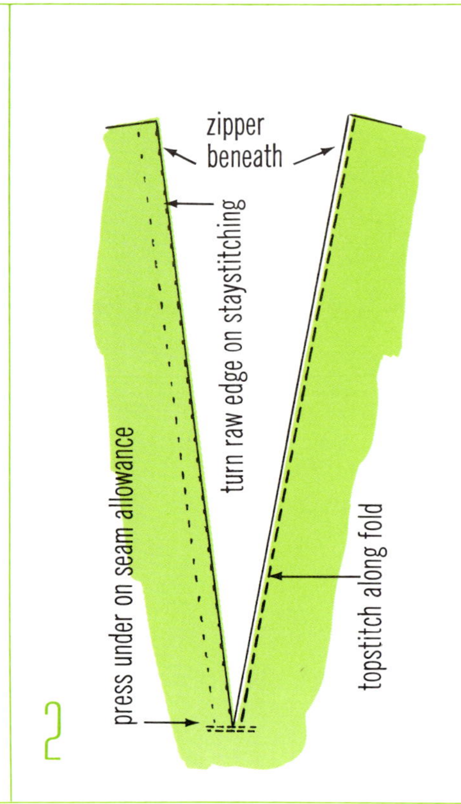

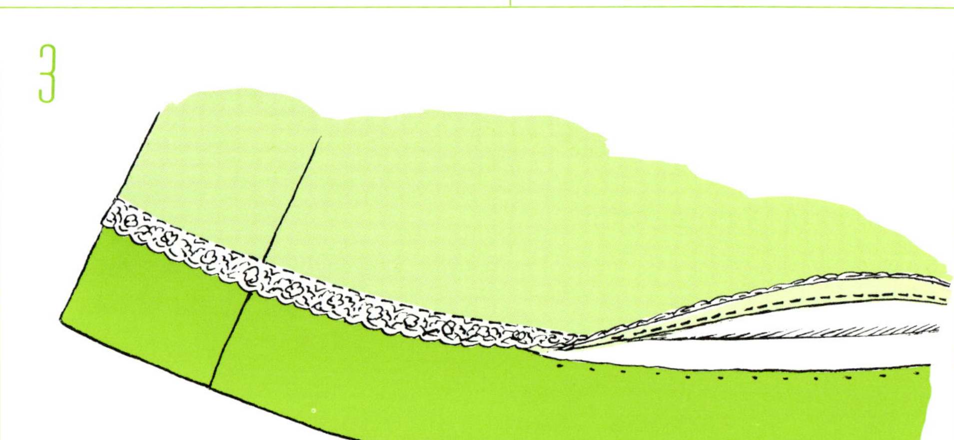

lining hem for full skirt
(rolled hem beneath lace)

☆ At the waistline the lining is enclosed inside the waistband.

For pants, keep these additional points in mind:

☆ With firmly woven fabrics, or to give more body to some knits you may wish to use tricot or nylon jersey, because of their suppleness and give. With these fabrics slipstitch the zipper opening to the garment opening.

☆ Instead of leaving lining free at hem or using a takeup tuck, cut lining to finished length of hem and turn up pants hem over lining.

☆ Enclose the lining in the waistband as for skirts.

☆ For a waistline with a fitted facing, cut and stitch lining to facing, as for dress neckline. See Method One and Method Two, pages 44–46.

LINED SKIRT OR PANTS WITH ELASTIC WAISTBAND

To line a knit skirt or pants with an elastic waistband, make the garment without a zipper and few if any darts. Cut the lining like the garment but 1 inch (2.5cm) shorter for skirt. For pants cut the lining to the hem foldline.

With right sides together, stitch lining to skirt/pants. Trim the seam; understitch, turn, and press it. Topstitch the seam ⅛ inch (3mm) from edge. Make a second row of topstitching ⅛ inch (3mm) plus the width of the elastic you will use [1⅛ inch (2.8cm) for 1-inch (2.5-cm) elastic].

Open one seam of the lining between the two rows of topstitching. Insert elastic. Try on garment, and adjust elastic to fit. Pin elastic. Leave a ½-inch (1.3-cm) lap and stitch elastic.

Leave lining of skirt free at hem. Finish lining hem by stitching a row of lace to raw edge. Lining hem, including lace, should end 1 inch (2.5cm) above hem foldline.

For pants turn up hem over lining and stitch hem edge to lining, using tailor's hem.

topstitching
lining, including lace, ends 1″ (2.5 cm) above hem foldline

IT'S ELEMENTARY

PREPARATION/CUTTING/MARKING/STITCHING 52

STITCHING GUIDES 60

PRESSING 65

PRESSING GUIDES 66

PREPARATION CUTTING MARKING STITCHING

GRAINLINE

Cutting, fitting, stitching, and pressing are directed to making a garment that is grain-perfect. Grain perfection is vital if a garment is to keep its shape and appearance, because grain always seeks its true position. A garment can hang, wear, and fit beautifully only when grain-perfect.

Warp yarns compose the lengthwise grain of the fabric; the filling, or weft, yarns make up the crosswise grain. If the warp and filling yarns lie at right angles to each other, the grain is true. If they do not lie at right angles, the fabric is off-grain.

Lengthwise grain of woven fabric is usually strongest and has the greatest amount of stability. Crosswise grain has a slight amount of give. True bias, which has the greatest amount of stretch, lies at a 45-degree angle to the true grain.

Knitted fabrics do not have warp and filling threads. The vertical rib of a knit fabric is called the wale; it is comparable to the crosswise grain of woven fabric. The greatest stretch in most knits is in the crosswise grain.

STRAIGHTEN ENDS OF FABRIC

If a garment is to be made on grain, the fabric must be on grain before the garment pieces are cut. The way to find if your fabric is on-grain and the first steps to straightening off-grain fabric are the same: Make each of the crosswise ends straight, with the end crosswise thread running from selvage to selvage. The method depends on fabric.

Many, but not all, fabrics can be torn. Linen, many wools, fabrics with heavy or rough threads, most nap-surfaced fabrics, and knits will not tear well.

If you have a fabric that will tear, clip a selvage with your scissors as far down as appears necessary to straighten the end. Hold each side of the clipped edge firmly, and give a quick pull. The fabric should tear across to the other selvage, which you then will need to cut across. It is necessary to tear quickly and firmly to avoid a lengthwise split in the material. If you have any doubts as to your success, use one of the other methods. Press raw edges to flatten ripples and restore grainline.

1 Drawing or pulling a thread is another way to straighten crosswise ends of fabric. Find a thread that goes all the way across; carefully pull it until the fabric puckers and you can see the threadline distinctly. Cut the fabric along this line to straighten each end.

On some fabrics it will not be possible to pull a thread all the way across, but you can ravel the crosswise threads until you have a straight thread across the width of fabric. Cut off raveled threads.

2 If a fabric has a woven design such as a plaid or crosswise stripe, cut along one of the lines of the design.

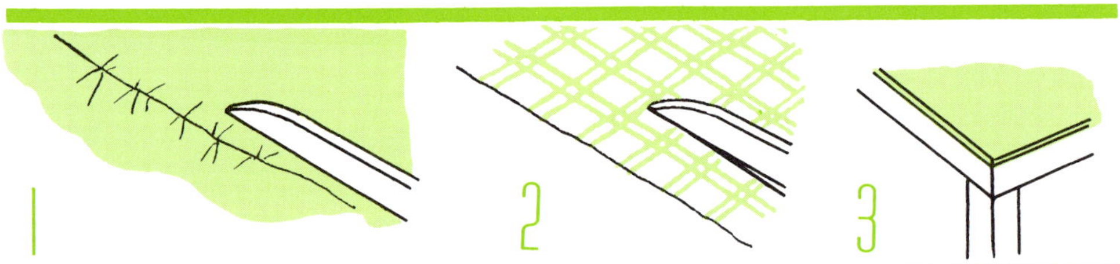

However, be sure that the fabric design is woven. Designs that are printed on fabric may be off grain.

To straighten the crosswise ends of a knit fabric, fold the fabric in half lengthwise, making sure the foldline is on a lengthwise rib. Use a T-square, or place the lengthwise grain against one side of a square table or your cutting board. Mark straight across the crosswise end with chalk, and cut along mark.

CHECK GRAIN POSITION When both ends of the fabric have been straightened, you will be able to determine the grain position of the threads. Fold the fabric lengthwise with the selvages together, smoothing the fabric toward the fold. Line up the selvage straight against the corner of a table. (You can also use the corner of your cutting board, or 3 the right angle of a T-square.) If the grain is straight, or true, one crosswise edge will lie straight against the other side of the right angle, the folded edge will lie flat, and the surface of the fabric will be smooth.

If this is not the case, you will need to straighten the fabric grain before cutting out the pattern pieces. In most cases straightening the grain can be combined with the process of preshrinking your fabric. After your fabric has been processed and the grain straightened, it should be kept folded accordion-fashion on the true grain until it is ready for use.

PRESHRINK FABRIC/STRAIGHTEN GRAIN It is a general rule that washable fabrics and most wools should be preshrunk before cutting. Prepare the fabric by perfecting the crosswise ends, then fold, right sides together, and baste the selvages and the two crosswise ends. The fabric is ready for preshrinking. This is an important step, because even a small amount of shrinkage can alter the fit of a garment enough to ruin the effect you are working to obtain. Remember to preshrink all other parts of a garment that will be laundered—interfacings, if woven, zippers, and any other notions.

If you will launder your garment, wash the fabric before cutting exactly as you will wash the completed garment. This means that you must read care labels carefully for information concerning the fabric and its performance. You must know at what temperatures your fabric can be washed and how to dry it.

Use the same soap you will use, and wash and dry the fabric at the same temperature as you will the garment. (The automatic dryer, as well as the washing process, can cause shrinkage.) If the garment is to be drip-dried and the fabric is a knit, be careful to support the length so it will not stretch. (The weight of a wet length of several yards of fabric will be much greater than that of your completed garment, and your garment will be supported by seams.) You can begin to press when the fabric is damp-dry if you need to straighten the grain.

If your fabric is washable but you intend to dryclean the garment (as you might linen, for example), prepare by basting; then press the fabric with a steam iron, straightening the grain, if necessary.

Although they will be drycleaned, all wool fabrics should be preshrunk, because steam pressing will shrink them. Some wools will have been preshrunk when you buy them. If your fabric has not been, preshrink it. If it is not grain-perfect, you will need to straighten the grain after preshrinking. Preshrink and straighten the grain as follows.

Baste the fabric, folded lengthwise with right sides together. Snip the selvages at intervals. Prepare processing cloths from old sheets or any clean, absorbent, nonfading cotton fabric that will hold moisture well. The cloths should be several inches wider than the fabric folded lengthwise, and they should be as long as the fabric. (To insure enough length several pieces can be sewed together, or they can simply be laid end to end, so long as the ends meet.) Wet these cloths thoroughly and remove excess water, leaving the cloths damp.

Use a large piece of plastic to protect the surface on which you lay the cloths. Spread the damp cloths over the plastic on a flat surface, and center the wool—folded lengthwise, right sides together, basted—on them. Fold wool and cloths together evenly from both ends toward the center in several folds. Press on the folds with your hands to be sure that the moisture penetrates the layers. Cover with the plastic to help retain and distribute the moisture. Leave for two to four hours; then remove the fabric, unfold, and lay it on a flat surface. Smooth and pull it gently with your hands until it is grain-perfect. When the wool is almost dry on one side, turn it to the other to shrink it evenly. Use steam to press on the lengthwise grain and straighten grain if necessary.

SHRINK NOTIONS Woven interfacings, belting, ribbons, trims, even zippers, if they are to be used on washable garments, should be preshrunk before the garment is made. Be sure they are wet thoroughly; then dry, and press if necessary.

FABRICS THAT NEED NOT BE PRESHRUNK An off-grain fabric that does not require preshrinking can often be straightened by steam pressing. Baste the two selvages together after your fabric has been folded lengthwise with the right sides together. Match the folded fabric at each end; then baste across the two matched ends. The fabric will not lie smoothly if it is off-grain.

Test press your fabric. See Pressing and pressing charts, pages 92–96. Dampen the fabric on the underside with a sponge or damp cloth, and press carefully along the lengthwise grain, moving from the selvage to the fold. Be careful not to press the fold; this would make a crease that would be difficult to remove. Smooth the fabric with your hands as you work, and keep the fabric square with the grain at all times. If the fabric is extremely off-grain, this method may not straighten it.

It may be easier to correct the grain on shorter lengths of fabric. Cut the fabric into lengths on which major pattern pieces will fit. This technique does not require more fabric, and it will help greatly to achieve grain perfection in cutting.

DOUBLE KNITS If a polyester double knit garment is to be washed, the fabric should be preshrunk. Polyester double knits to be drycleaned need not be. To straighten double knits straighten the crosswise ends; baste; then straighten the grain as for a woven fabric, by pressing. Be sure your iron is at the right setting for your fabric when pressing.

LAMINATED KNITS AND FABRICS WITH PERMANENT FINISHES Laminated knits, commonly called bonded knits, and fabrics with permanent press or crease-resistant finishes, polished cottons, and chintzes will have threads locked in a permanent position. If these are off-grain, they cannot be straightened. If you use such a fabric, place the straight-of-the-grain markings of the pattern on the straight of the design rather than the grainline. Do this for each individual pattern piece. If the fabric does not have a design, sometimes you can align each pattern piece separately on the straight of grain.

Permanent finishes with a fishy smell should be washed with a detergent in a regular wash cycle.

CUTTING AND MARKING

Cutting-to-fit is a technique for altering the measurement of your garment pieces to fit while cutting out the fabric. See pages 97–102. If you must alter your pattern, take this into consideration while laying out pattern pieces in order to allow the necessary additional inches for each garment piece that you must alter.

Lay out and check all the pattern pieces against the layout guide. Be sure you have allowed space for any necessary alterations. When cutting knits use the wale of the fabric as the lengthwise grain. If a knit has a fold that cannot be pressed out, place your pattern pieces in such a way as to avoid the fold, or place it on a part of the garment—under the arm, for example—where it will not be conspicuous.

It is helpful to cut extra notches on pattern and fabric pieces. The top of the sleevecap by the shoulder seam mark and the center fold of a shirt back that will be joined to a yoke are two examples of places where extra notches are useful.

Use tracing paper and wheel to transfer pattern marks to the wrong side of garment pieces, and use thread tracing (basting through a single layer) for marks that must be visible on right side of garment.

MACHINE STITCHING

Regulation stitches are used for the permanent stitching of seams, darts, and other garment details. The length of permanent stitches can vary depending on the fabric. See charts, pages 87–91, for suggested stitch length for various fabrics.

Staystitching is regulation-length stitching done in the direction of the grain before a garment piece is joined to another. It is usually done a thread outside the seamline, in the seam allowance, unless instructions call for stitching at a different distance from the seam. Staystitching is used on any area of a garment that is more than slightly off-grain or that requires further construction. It prevents these edges of garment pieces from stretching during construction.

Baste stitching is done with the longest machine stitch (6–8). It is used to hold two layers of fabric together before permanent stitching them. You may want to do this for fitting a garment. Basting is also useful in difficult areas of construction, or if fabric is hard to stitch for some reason. Basting is sometimes used as a guide for other stitching.

Grain direction can usually be seen
1 by the position of fabric threads at raw edges. The threads lie smooth and straight along cut edges in direction of the grain. Against the grain they appear curled back, rough, and uneven. Basting, staystitching, and regulation stitching should be done in direction of the grain, except for edges that are cut on the straight or almost-straight of either lengthwise or crosswise grain.
2 These can be stitched in either direction. See the illustrations for directional stitching to maintain true grain in your garment pieces.

STAYSTITCH PLUS This may need practice to master, but it is useful in fitting the hem edge of a flared or A-line skirt to underside of skirt for hemming, in easing the back of a sleeve to front at elbow, or in easing a back shoulder to front shoulder of a garment where required.

Use a regular-length stitch, and press index finger of right hand firmly against back of presser foot as you sew. Threads of the fabric are 3 crowded together as fabric piles up against the finger. Release fabric, and repeat until the area that requires easing has been stitched.

HAND STITCHES

Choose needle and thread. To thread a needle, cut thread at an angle with sharp scissors. This makes a clean, sharp end that goes through the eye of the needle easily. Always work with a single strand of thread. Coat thread with beeswax, and run a warm iron over it to keep it from knotting. Thread needle with end of thread that was cut from spool. The same end should be knotted before beginning to sew.

BAR TACKS Bar tacks can be made by hand, as well as by machine. To make them by hand, take 4 three or four stitches of the length required in the same place, inserting needle through fabric each time. Then, beginning at one end of the long stitches, take small overhand stitches over the three or four threads, catching some of the fabric underneath as you do so, until the first stitches are entirely covered. Finish each end of the bar with a smaller bar stitched perpendicular to it if you like.

BASTING Hand basting can be used instead of machine basting when a delicate fabric is apt to show 5 marks from machine basting. Use thread of a contrasting color and large, straight stitches. Stitch a thread outside the seamline in the seam allowance. At the beginning and end of stitching use short backstitches to secure basting. A variation is a long stitch on one side of fabric and a short on the other.

1

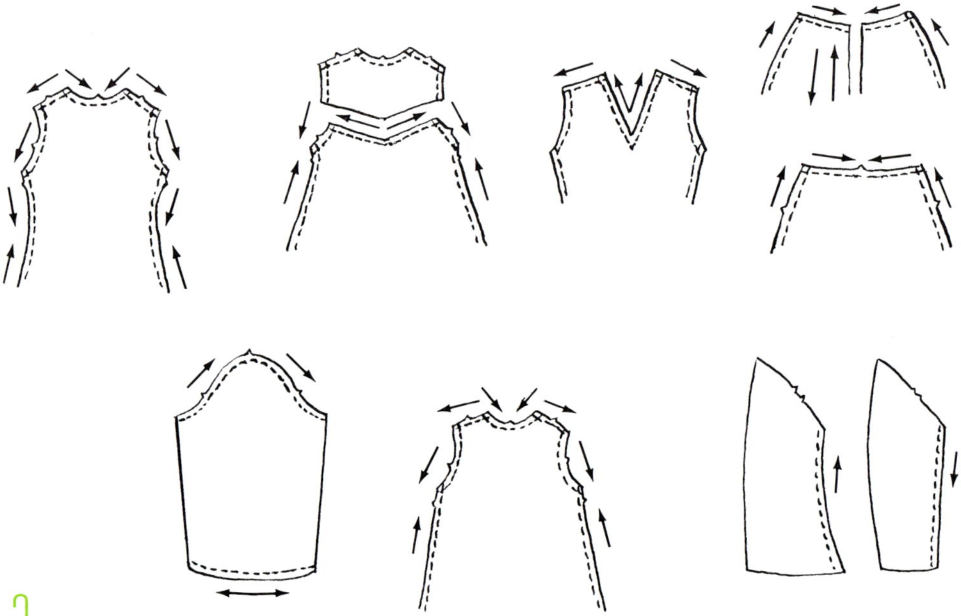

2

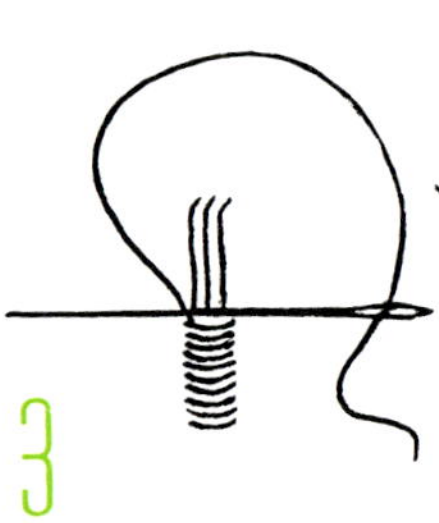

3

4

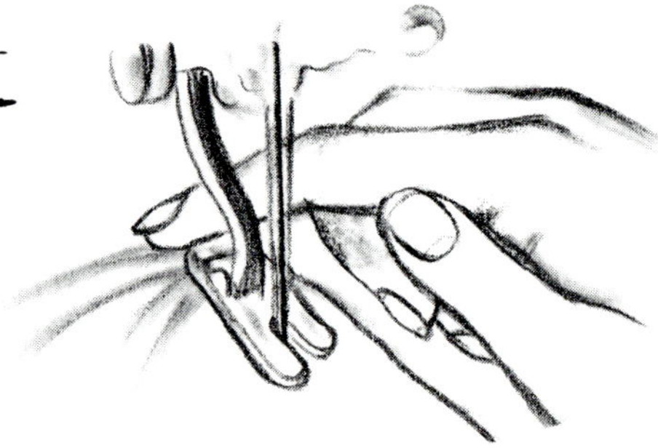

5

1 OVERCAST Overcasting can be used to keep raw edges of seams from raveling. Stitch at a slant, using large, even, closely spaced stitches.

2 RUNNING STITCH The length of these stitches will depend on the fabric and on the purpose of the stitches. To hand stitch sheer or delicate fabrics, use a 1/16-inch (1.5-mm) stitch. For medium to heavy fabrics, use a 1/8-inch (3-mm) stitch. Use a 1/4-inch (6-mm) stitch for hand gathering. Insert needle in fabric, push it through with thimble, and draw thread through. Be sure to keep fabric flat, and do not allow thread to pucker fabric. Repeat procedure.

3 SLIPSTITCH The slipstitch can be used to join two edges without the stitches showing; however, it is not a strong stitch and should not be used in an area that will be subject to strain. For hems, it will scarcely be visible on the garment or the hem side. (Do not use it for hems with heavy fabrics.) Insert needle first into underside of hem fold and then into garment, picking up only a single thread in the garment side. Draw needle and thread through; repeat.

WHIPSTITCH The whipstitch is stronger than the slipstitch and can be substituted for it to hold together edges that will be subject to strain. It might be used to attach inside edges of cuffs to sleeves, or the center back of a collar to a shirt when the fabric is bulky or heavy or when the garment will receive hard wear.

4 Insert needle through upper edge, hiding knot beneath edge. Place point of needle in opposite side, as

1

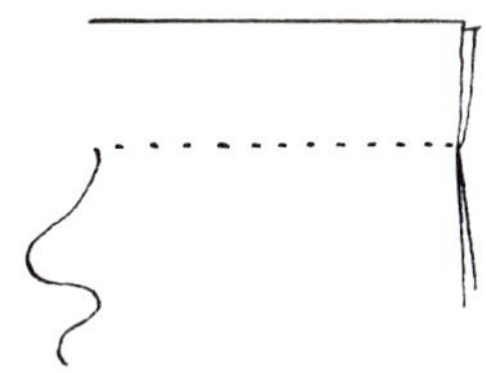

2

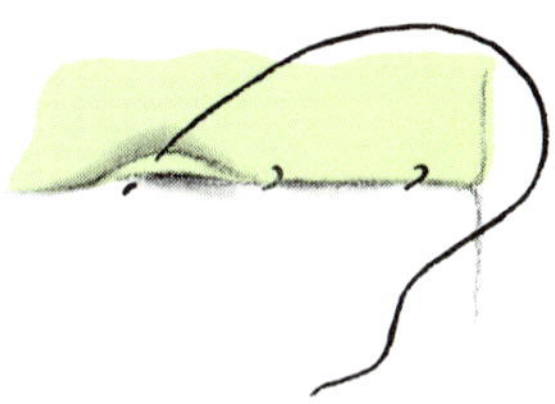

3

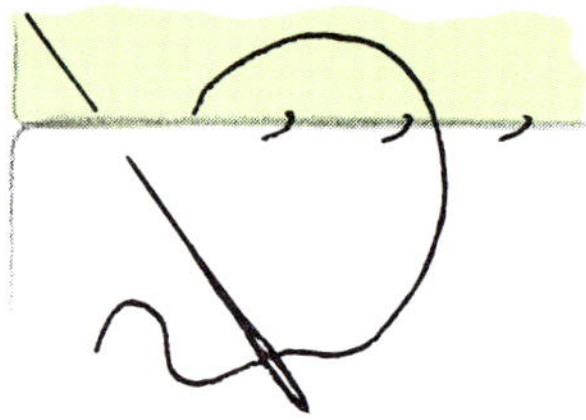

4

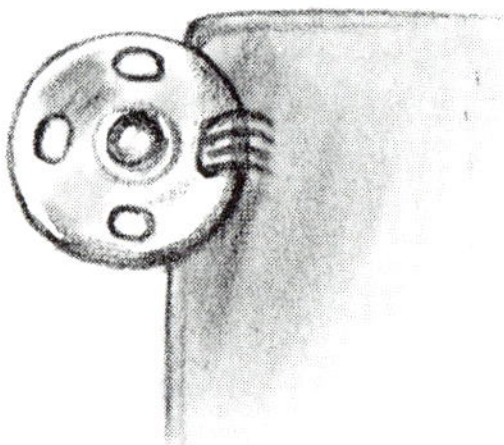

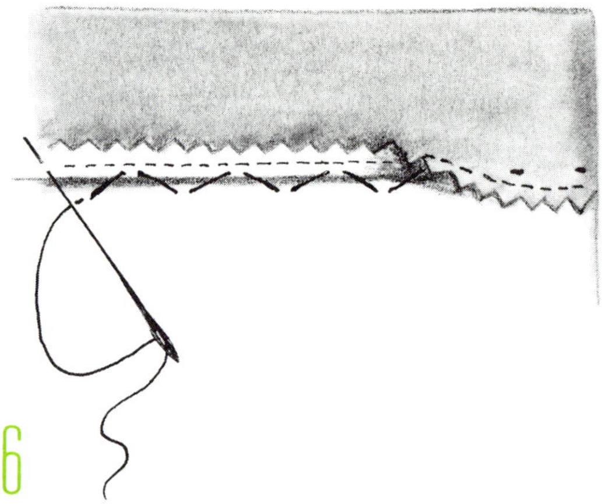

5

6

near as possible to the first edge. With point of needle under edge, move needle ahead, bringing it up through the first edge. Repeat procedure. The stitches should be so small they scarcely can be seen.

5 HANGING SNAP A hanging snap may be used on the edge of a garment like a hook and eye, but only in an area that does not have great strain. The socket half of snap is attached to the inside overlap of the garment closing in the same way a plain snap is attached. The ball half is attached to the other side of closing underlap through one hole only.

If extra give is needed to make closing easier, add a thread shank.

TAILOR'S HEM This is a method of stitching very often used on hems, regardless of how the hem edge is finished. Stitches are concealed between the wrong sides of skirt and hem. In most cases, garment and hem should face you, with hem turned back about ¼ inch. (On some delicate fabrics in which creases may be difficult to press out, it is better to hold garment and hem away from you, and just turn back top of hem.) Work from right to left. Space stitches no more than ½ inch apart for a secure hem. 6

FABRIC	NEEDLE	THREAD	STITCH LENGTH
CORDUROY AND VELVETEEN	14	mercerized	8–10 per inch
CREPE	11	mercerized; silk for topstitching	10–12
DENIM	14, 16	heavy duty mercerized	8–12
DOUBLE KNIT	11, 14 sharp or ball-point	mercerized. . . . . . . .machine stretch poly/cot*, polyester. . . .zigzag or regular all, 10–12	
DURABLE PRESS	11–14	mercerized or poly/cot*	heavy, 8–10 light, 10–14
FELT	14, sharp	mercerized	8–10
JERSEY	9–11, sharp or ball-point	polyester or poly/cot*	12–14
LACE	11	mercerized, poly/cot,* or silk, according to fabric	10–12
LEATHER AND SUEDE	leather 11–16	heavy-duty mercerized, polyester, or silk	8–10
LEATHERLIKE AND VINYL	leather 14–16	polyester poly/cot*	8–10

* Polyester/cotton

† NOTES FOR SPECIAL HANDLING

1. Use a roller foot.
2. Stitch with tissue paper between presser foot and fabric.
3. Stitch with tissue between throatplate and fabric.
4. Cover the throatplate hole with a piece of adhesive tape.
5. Place a piece of adhesive or cellophane tape around the toes of your regular presser foot.
6. With a zigzag or straight stitch, hold the fabric in front and in back of the presser foot firmly enough to stretch it (keep it taut) as you sew. Hold the fabric to its true maximum length without stretching out of shape. You will not need this technique if you have a stretch stitch on your machine. Sometimes a fine zigzag stitch with polyester thread will provide enough give. Make a sample seam, and stretch it. If the stitching breaks, you need to stretch as you sew.

TENSION	PRESSURE	† NOTES FOR SPECIAL HANDLING	SEAM FINISH
slightly relaxed	average, but test	11, 12	edgestitch
relaxed, but test	light	10, 12	zigzag or overcast
average	average to heavy	no special handling needed	no, unless flat-fell
average	average	6, 7	no
usually slightly relaxed	average, but test	3 or 4; 8	sometimes; pink or zigzag
slightly increased	slightly increased	13	no
test	average	3 or 4; 6	no, but edgestitch seams that roll
slightly relaxed	test	5, 10	French or mock French if seam will show
slightly relaxed	fairly light	7, 9, 13	glue or topstitch
average to slightly increased	light to average	1 or 2; 3, 13, 14	topstitch or glue (note difference for Suedelike, next page)

7. Stay seams that should not stretch—waistline or shoulder seams—with a piece of seam tape or yarn.
8. Hold fabric firmly in front and in back of the presser foot.
9. Be careful not to stretch while stitching.
10. Use both hands—one behind the presser foot to guide, not pull, the fabric under the needle.
11. Use your hand to separate the fabric layers in front of the needle.
12. Fabric may be slippery, or it may push ahead on the top layer. To prevent, baste before stitching.
13. Stitch carefully. If you baste, do so just in the seam allowance. The needle holes will not disappear if you remove stitching.
14. A special stitching tape with adhesive on one side and rows of parallel lines on the other is useful for topstitching. Stitch through tape, following lines; then remove tape when stitching is completed.

FABRIC	NEEDLE	THREAD	STITCH LENGTH
QIANA	11	polyester poly/cot* silk "A"	wovens, 10–12 more for knits
SATIN	11	mercerized polyester silk	12
SHEERS	9–11	fine	16
SILK	11	silk	light, 12–16 medium, 10–14
SUEDELIKE	leather 14–16	polyester silk	10–12, seams 5–8, ornamental
TRICOT	sharp or ball-point 9–11	polyester	12–15; fine, narrow zigzag, or 2 rows straight stitching
VELVET	11	mercerized silk	10–12; stitch in direction of nap

*Polyester/cotton

† NOTES FOR SPECIAL HANDLING

1. Use a roller foot.
2. Stitch with tissue paper between presser foot and fabric.
3. Stitch with tissue between throatplate and fabric.
4. Cover the throatplate hole with a piece of adhesive tape.
5. Place a piece of adhesive or cellophane tape around the toes of your regular presser foot.
6. With a zigzag or straight stitch, hold the fabric in front and in back of the presser foot firmly enough to stretch it (keep it taut) as you sew. Hold the fabric to its true maximum length without stretching out of shape. You will not need this technique if you have a stretch stitch on your machine. Sometimes a fine zigzag stitch with polyester thread will provide enough give. Make a sample seam, and stretch it. If the stitching breaks, you need to stretch as you sew.

TENSION	PRESSURE	†NOTES FOR SPECIAL HANDLING	SEAM FINISH
average	test	8	no
slightly relaxed	light	8, 13	if ravels, zigzag or overcast
light to average	light	soft sheers: 2 and/or 3; 10	French or mock French
usually slightly relaxed	light	12 and sometimes 13	sometimes: pink or zigzag
relaxed	test	1, 13; 2 for topstitching	do not use glue; topstitch or use heat-fusible adhesives
usually slightly relaxed	average	1, 4, 6	trim and stitch seam allowances together
usually slightly relaxed	light to average	12	no (garment should be lined)

7. Stay seams that should not stretch—waistline or shoulder seams—with a piece of seam tape or yarn.
8. Hold fabric firmly in front and in back of the presser foot.
9. Be careful not to stretch while stitching.
10. Use both hands—one behind the presser foot to guide, not pull, the fabric under the needle.
11. Use your hand to separate the fabric layers in front of the needle.
12. Fabric may be slippery, or it may push ahead on the top layer. To prevent, baste before stitching.
13. Stitch carefully. If you baste, do so just in the seam allowance. The needle holes will not disappear if you remove stitching.
14. A special stitching tape with adhesive on one side and rows of parallel lines on the other is useful for topstitching. Stitch through tape, following lines; then remove tape when stitching is completed.

If your fabric is not listed in the stitching charts, use the following as a general guide for needle, thread, and stitch length. To learn if any special handling is necessary, make a sample seam and observe how the fabric behaves.

FABRIC WEIGHT	VERY LIGHT	LIGHT	MEDIUM	MEDIUM HEAVY	HEAVY
EXAMPLE	ciré	gingham	linen	flannel	duck
NEEDLE	9	9, 11	11, 14	14, 16	16, 18
STITCH LENGTH	16–20	12–16	10–14	8–12	6–10
MERCERIZED COTTON	fine	50	50	50 or heavy duty	heavy duty
SILK	"A"	"A"	"A"	"A"	
POLYESTER/COTTON	X	X	X	X	X
POLYESTER	X	X	X	heavy duty	heavy duty
NYLON		nylon tricot	X	X	X

Note: An X indicates that the appropriate thread comes in only one size.

PRESSING

There are several basic rules to observe when pressing. The first is always test press a scrap of your fabric to determine the most effective temperature and see if the fabric shows iron shine or if it waterspots. You can avoid possible damage to your fashion fabric by taking a few minutes for test pressing.

Remember never to slide the iron across fabric. Lift the iron and set it down when you move it from one area to another. Always press with the grain to avoid distortion of garment lines. This is as important as preparing, cutting, and stitching the fabric on grain.

Use steam for construction pressing except when fiber or fabric prohibits. In cases where it is not possible to raise steam in the iron with the temperature setting required by the fiber or fabric, a dampened (never wet) press cloth can be used between the iron and fabric to provide moisture. A dampened press or cheesecloth can also be used to supply extra moisture as needed.

In addition to a drill press cloth, one of self-fabric is useful for pressing napped fabrics. There are some cases in which brown paper or tissue paper are useful as substitutes for a press cloth. In the case of silk, tissue paper can be used between iron and fabric to prevent waterspotting. Brown paper strips or strips of paper toweling should be used between such construction details as seam allowances, tucks, darts, and the fabric when pressing a fabric that marks easily. This helps prevent marks of the construction from showing on the right side of the garment.

The pounding block is used to pound steam into heavy fabric to mold it, and for flattening seams, pleats, and edges in heavy and resilient fabrics such as wool.

For leather and suede use brown paper over and under the fabric when you press. The top layer protects the fabric, and the paper underneath prevents small pieces of rough leather from clinging to your press board.

An attachment for irons is available at notions counters. It eliminates the need for a pressing cloth with synthetic fabrics. It keeps the hot metal soleplate from direct contact with fabric, and can be used with steam or dry iron. Be sure to test press your fabric in any case.

The following charts give general rules for pressing fabrics. There are two parts. You will need to consult both because either or both fiber and fabric construction may require or restrict heat, moisture, or other conditions. This will determine how to press your fabric, but it is not a substitute for test pressing.

To use the chart as a guide, use all the procedures for pressing fiber or fabric construction by standard method (black circles and type) or an alternate method (colored circles and type). Colored and black circles in a single square indicate a procedure used in both methods. Try method on a scrap of fabric.

FIBER			NO HEAT		HEAT				
	RIGHT SIDE	WRONG SIDE	FINGER PRESS	MALLET	VERY LOW	MEDIUM LOW	LOW	MEDIUM	HIGH
ACETATE	○	●			●○				
ACRYLIC		●				●			
COTTON	*	●							●
LINEN		●							●
NYLON		●	○		●				
NYLON BLENDS		●			SEE CARE LABEL				
POLYESTER		●						●	
QIANA	○	●						●	
RAYON		●				●			
SILK		●						●	
TRIACETATE		●				●			
VINYL/PLASTIC	***		●	○					
WOOL		●						●	

● STANDARD METHOD
○ ALTERNATE METHOD
●○ BOTH METHODS

SEE TEXT FOR DETAILS

PRESSING GUIDE

STEAM	DRY	POUNDING BLOCK	TENSION	PROTECTION						
				OVER FABRIC				UNDER FABRIC		
				PRESS CLOTH	PAPER STRIPS	TISSUE PAPER	BROWN PAPER	HEAVY TOWEL	NEEDLEBOARD	SELF-FABRIC
●				D						
●				D						
●	★			★						
●				●						
●				D						
TEST				●						
●				●						
● ●			●	●						
●				●						
●				●		★★				
●				●						
	●									
●		●		●						

D/D Use dampened press cloth to steam press.

★ After steam pressing cotton, press until dry with dry iron; use press cloth when top pressing dark or textured cotton.

★★ Tissue may be needed under press cloth to prevent waterspotting.

★★★ Some vinyl and plastic-coated fabrics may be top pressed with a warm iron over a press cloth; see care label.

FABRIC CONSTRUCTION	RIGHT SIDE	WRONG SIDE	NO HEAT		HEAT				
			FINGER PRESS	MALLET	VERY LOW	MEDIUM LOW	LOW	MEDIUM	HIGH
CORDUROY/VELVETEEN		●			SEE FIBER				
CREPE		●			SEE FIBER				
DURABLE PRESS	*	●					●		*
DENIM		●			SEE FIBER				
FELT		●						●	
KNITS		●			SEE FIBER				
LACE		●			SEE FIBER				
LAMINATED/BONDED	●		● (green)		SEE FIBER				
LEATHER/SUEDE		● ● (green)		● (green)		●			
LEATHERLIKE/VINYL		●	●	● (green)	**				
NAPPED		●			SEE FIBER				
SATIN		●			SEE FIBER				
SUEDELIKE		●				●			
VELVET		●			SEE FIBER				

● STANDARD METHOD

● (green) ALTERNATE METHOD

● ● (green) BOTH METHODS

SEE TEXT FOR DETAILS

STEAM	DRY	PROTECTION							
		OVER FABRIC				UNDER FABRIC			
		PRESS CLOTH	PAPER STRIPS	TISSUE PAPER	BROWN PAPER	HEAVY TOWEL	NEEDLEBOARD	BROWN PAPER	SELF-FABRIC
●		●				●	●		● (green)
	●	●				●			
★	●		●						
●									
	●	●	●						
●		●	●						
TEST		SEE FIBER				●			
●		●	●		● (green)			●	
	●	● (green)			●			●	
	★★	★★							
●	●	●				●			● (green)
TEST									
●		★★★	●			●			
●		★★★★					●		

★ When final pressing use highest temperature fiber will take and lots of steam.
★★ Some vinyls can be pressed on right side with a warm iron over a presscloth; see care label.
★★★ Use a mesh press cloth; press marks usually can be brushed off.
★★★★ Hold iron about 1 inch (2.5cm.) above fabric.

INDEX

armholes
  inserting lining,38–39,41–44
  interfacing at,25

bar tacks,56
basting,56
  for fitting,14,36,38
bias collar,25–26
bias, true,52
brown paper for pressing,66

collars
  bias,25–26
  rolled,30–31
  standing,25–29
cutting-to-fit,55

darts,12–13

elastic waistbands,48

fabric
  charts for pressing,66–69
  charts for stitching,60–64
  choosing,7,32
  heavyweight,10,12,14,16,58,64
  lightweight,5,58,64
  preshrinking,53–55
  straightening grain of,52–53

fabric construction, pressing guide for (charts),68–69
fibers, pressing guide for (charts), 66–67
fitting,36,38

grain
  stitching with,56–57
  straightening,52–55

hanging snap,59
heavyweight fabrics
  hems for,16
  stitch length for,58
  stitching (chart),64
  underlining for,10,12,14
hems,7,19,58,59
  for linings,35,38,44–46
  for underlinings,16–18

interfacing
  for armholes,25
  for collar,25–28,30
  for neckline,24
  preshrinking,53–54

knits
  grain of,52
  linings for,32
  preshrinking,55
  straightening grain of,53,55

lightweight fabrics
  stitch length for,58
  stitching (chart),64
  underlinings for,5
linings,32–35,83
  at armholes,38–39,41–42,44
  choosing,32
  for garments with elastic waistbands,48
  hems for,35,38,44,46
  at neckline,39,41–46
  for pants and skirts,46–48
  stitching at zipper openings,39,40, 42–43,46

neckline finishes
  with lining,39,41–46
  with underlining,24
notions, preshrinking,53,54

overcast stitch,58

pants
  lining,46–48
  underlining,18–19
pattern
  laying out,55
  strengthening,8
pattern markings, transferring,8,55
permanent (regulation) stitching,55
preshrinking,53–55
press cloths,66
pressing,66
  construction,66
  final,18
  steam,66
  to straighten grain,54–55
  underlining,9–10,12
  use of pounding block in,66
pressing guide (charts),66–69

running stitch,58

skirts
  lining,46–48
  underlining,18–19
sleeves,18,20
  lining,36
slippage,10
slipstitching,58
snap, hanging,59
staystitching,55–56
stitch length (chart),64

stitches, hand,56–59
stitching guide,60–64
stitching, machine,55–56

takeup tuck,44
thread for stitching (charts),60–64
true bias,52
turn-of-cloth
  for collar,28
  for underlining,10

underlining,5–8
  attaching to garment,9–12
  darts in,12–13
  for dresses,21–22
  hems for,16–18,19
  with neckline interfacing,24
  for pants and skirts,18–19
  partial,21–23
  at shoulders,18,20

warp (lengthwise grain),52
weft (crosswise grain),52
whipstitching,58–59

zippers
  final pressing,18
  stitching linings at,40,42,43,46